PYTHON FOR
MACHINE LEARNING

Implement ML Models with
Scikit-Learn

THOMPSON CARTER

TABLE OF CONTENTS

Introduction

Python for Machine Learning: Implement ML Models with Scikit-Learn"

Welcome to **"Python for Machine Learning: Implement ML Models with Scikit-Learn"**! Whether you're just getting started with machine learning or looking to deepen your understanding of its implementation using Python, this book is designed to guide you through the essentials of building and deploying machine learning models from start to finish. With a focus on **Scikit-Learn**, one of the most widely used machine learning libraries in Python, you will gain hands-on experience in a wide range of machine learning tasks—ensuring that you're ready to tackle real-world challenges using powerful and efficient tools.

In today's rapidly evolving tech landscape, **machine learning (ML)** has become an essential part of virtually every industry. From predicting customer churn to enhancing product recommendations and automating decision-making processes, machine learning enables organizations to analyze vast amounts of data and derive actionable insights. However, transitioning from learning concepts to actually applying machine learning can be daunting. This book bridges that gap by providing practical, real-world examples and an approachable, jargon-free explanation of complex topics.

This book is structured in a way that ensures you understand the fundamental principles of machine learning while also learning how to implement them effectively using Python. If you have basic programming knowledge in Python and are comfortable with the concept of data analysis, you're ready to dive into this journey. Each chapter has been crafted to be clear, concise, and engaging, providing you with everything from foundational theory to advanced techniques.

What You Will Learn in This Book

- **Understanding Machine Learning**: We begin with an overview of what machine learning is, how it works, and how it differs from traditional programming. You will explore various types of machine learning, including **supervised**, **unsupervised**, and **reinforcement learning**, with an emphasis on supervised learning, which is most commonly used in real-world applications.
- **Python Libraries for ML**: Python is home to a rich ecosystem of libraries that make machine learning easier to implement. You will learn how to use libraries such as **NumPy**, **Pandas**, **Matplotlib**, **Seaborn**, and of course, **Scikit-learn**. These libraries provide the foundation for data manipulation, visualization, and the application of machine learning algorithms.

- **Scikit-Learn and ML Models**: Scikit-learn is the cornerstone of this book. We will take a deep dive into its functionality, helping you understand how to load datasets, train models, and evaluate their performance. You will work with a variety of machine learning algorithms, including **linear regression**, **decision trees**, **logistic regression**, **support vector machines (SVMs)**, and **k-nearest neighbors (k-NN)**, among others.

- **Data Preprocessing and Feature Engineering**: Effective data preparation is a critical step in building robust models. We will cover essential techniques for **data cleaning**, **handling missing values**, **feature scaling**, and **feature engineering**, enabling you to transform raw data into a form suitable for modeling.

- **Model Evaluation and Improvement**: Understanding how to evaluate and improve your models is just as important as building them. We will guide you through key metrics such as **accuracy**, **precision**, **recall**, **F1-score**, and more. You'll also learn how to perform **cross-validation**, handle overfitting and underfitting, and use **hyperparameter tuning** to enhance model performance.

- **Unsupervised Learning**: While supervised learning is a major focus, unsupervised learning is equally important, particularly for tasks like **clustering** and **dimensionality reduction**. You'll explore techniques such as **k-means**

clustering, **hierarchical clustering**, and **principal component analysis (PCA)**.

- **Deep Learning**: For those interested in the cutting-edge of machine learning, we'll also introduce deep learning concepts and how neural networks function. We'll briefly touch on how to build simple neural networks using **Keras** and **TensorFlow**.

- **Deploying Machine Learning Models**: Finally, we conclude the book by showing you how to take your machine learning models to production. You'll learn how to create APIs using **Flask** and deploy models to the cloud, enabling you to serve predictions to end-users in real-time.

Real-World Applications

Throughout the book, you will encounter real-world examples that illustrate how machine learning can be applied in diverse industries. These case studies range from predicting customer churn, employee turnover, and sales forecasting, to analyzing purchase behavior, segmenting customers, and classifying images or emails. Each chapter ties theoretical concepts to practical, business-oriented applications, helping you understand how the methods and techniques you learn can be used to solve real problems.

For instance, in the chapter on **logistic regression**, you'll learn how to predict whether a customer will buy a product or not based on demographic data. In the **clustering** chapter, we will explore how to use k-means clustering to segment customers based on purchasing patterns. This focus on practical applications ensures that the knowledge you gain can be directly applied to your own data science and machine learning projects.

Why This Book is Jargon-Free and Accessible

While machine learning can be a highly technical field, this book aims to break down complex concepts in simple, understandable language. We emphasize clarity and step-by-step guidance throughout each chapter. Rather than focusing on mathematical formulas and dense theory, we focus on what matters most: understanding the intuition behind the algorithms and knowing how to implement them effectively.

Real-world examples are presented in a straightforward manner, with easy-to-follow code snippets and explanations. This makes the content highly accessible, whether you're a beginner or someone who already has some experience in machine learning. You'll get to work on coding exercises that simulate realistic scenarios, ensuring you not only grasp the theory but also develop practical skills for real-world projects.

Who Should Read This Book?

This book is ideal for:

- **Beginner to Intermediate Python Programmers**: If you're comfortable with Python and want to dive deeper into the world of machine learning, this book will guide you from the basics to more advanced techniques.
- **Aspiring Data Scientists**: Whether you're looking to break into the field of data science or advance your existing knowledge, this book provides the foundational skills required to work with machine learning models.
- **Developers Interested in Machine Learning**: If you already have a programming background and want to transition into machine learning, this book provides you with the necessary tools to get started quickly.
- **Anyone Interested in Machine Learning Applications**: Whether you're a business analyst, marketer, or product manager, this book will help you understand how machine learning models can be applied to your domain to solve real-world problems.

Machine learning is a transformative technology that is changing industries across the globe. By learning to build and deploy machine learning models using Python and Scikit-learn, you are positioning yourself to be at the forefront of this revolution. This book is your practical guide to mastering the tools and techniques needed to create powerful machine learning applications, from training and evaluating models to deploying them into real-world environments. Whether you are building predictive models, conducting data analysis, or developing innovative solutions, the skills you will gain from this book are valuable in today's data-driven world.

Let's begin your journey into the world of machine learning!

Chapter 1: Introduction to Python for Machine Learning

Overview of Python's Role in Machine Learning

Python has become the de facto programming language for machine learning (ML), and it is widely favored by data scientists, machine learning engineers, and researchers for several reasons:

- **Simplicity**: Python's syntax is easy to learn and read, making it a great choice for beginners and professionals alike. It has a clean, readable code style that encourages rapid development and collaboration.
- **Large Ecosystem of Libraries**: Python boasts a rich ecosystem of libraries and frameworks that make machine learning implementation much easier. Some of the most popular libraries include:
    - **NumPy**: For numerical computing and working with arrays.
    - **pandas**: For data manipulation and analysis.
    - **Matplotlib & Seaborn**: For data visualization.
    - **Scikit-learn**: For implementing machine learning algorithms.
    - **TensorFlow, Keras, PyTorch**: For deep learning models.

- **Community Support**: Python has a massive global community, which means continuous improvement of its ecosystem, extensive documentation, and a wealth of tutorials, forums, and resources.
- **Interoperability**: Python integrates well with other technologies and tools, allowing data scientists to work seamlessly in different environments and frameworks.
- **Versatility**: Python is not only used for machine learning but also for web development, data analysis, automation, scientific computing, and more, making it an all-around tool in the data science toolkit.

Machine learning, which involves building models to identify patterns and make predictions from data, requires effective data manipulation, analysis, and visualization capabilities. Python, with its libraries, makes these tasks efficient and manageable. It's also capable of scaling with the complexity of ML models, from simpler algorithms like linear regression to more sophisticated techniques like deep learning.

Installing Python, Setting Up Environments, and Introduction to Jupyter Notebooks

Before diving into machine learning with Python, you need to set up your environment. This chapter walks you through the steps of installing Python and setting up the essential tools for developing machine learning models.

1. Installing Python

To get started with Python for machine learning, follow these steps:

1. **Install Python**:
   - Download the latest version of Python from the official website.
   - Make sure to select the option to "Add Python to PATH" during the installation process, which makes Python accessible from the command line.

2. **Install Anaconda** (optional but recommended):
   - **Anaconda** is a Python distribution that includes Python, popular machine learning libraries, and development tools like Jupyter notebooks.
   - It simplifies the management of Python libraries and environments.
   - Download and install Anaconda from the official site.

    o Anaconda comes with **conda**, a package manager for installing and managing packages and virtual environments.

2. Setting Up Virtual Environments

A **virtual environment** allows you to isolate dependencies for different projects, preventing conflicts between package versions. Using `venv` (or `conda` for Anaconda users), you can create an isolated environment for your Python project.

- **Using venv** (for standard Python installation):
    1. Create a virtual environment:

    ```bash
    python -m venv myenv
    ```

    2. Activate the virtual environment:
        - On Windows:

        ```bash
        myenv\Scripts\activate
        ```

        - On macOS/Linux:

        ```bash
        source myenv/bin/activate
        ```

- **Using Conda** (for Anaconda users):
  1. Create a virtual environment:

     ```bash
     bash
     ```

     ```bash
     conda create --name myenv python=3.x
     ```

  2. Activate the environment:

     ```bash
     bash
     ```

     ```bash
     conda activate myenv
     ```

3. Installing Necessary Libraries

Once you have your environment set up, you can install the libraries you'll need for machine learning. The most essential libraries are:

- **Scikit-learn**: The main library for machine learning in Python.
- **pandas**: For data manipulation and analysis.
- **NumPy**: For numerical operations and working with arrays.
- **Matplotlib & Seaborn**: For plotting and data visualization.

Use the following commands to install these libraries:

```bash
bash
```

```
pip install scikit-learn pandas numpy matplotlib
seaborn
```

Or, if you're using conda:

```bash
```

```
conda install scikit-learn pandas numpy matplotlib
seaborn
```

4. Installing Jupyter Notebooks

Jupyter Notebooks are an interactive development environment that allows you to write and execute Python code in a browser-based interface. It's particularly useful for data science, as it allows you to document your analysis alongside the code and visualizations.

To install Jupyter Notebooks:

```bash
```

```
pip install notebook
```

Or, using conda:

```bash
```

```
conda install jupyter
```

Once installed, you can start a Jupyter notebook session by running:

```bash
```

```
jupyter notebook
```

This will open a browser window where you can create and work with notebooks.

Real-World Example: Setting Up the Environment for a Data Science Project

Now that you've installed Python and set up your environment, let's walk through setting up the environment for a typical data science project focused on **predicting customer churn**.

1. Create a Project Folder

Create a folder on your computer where you will store all project-related files (e.g., data, code, notebooks, and models). Name it something like `customer_churn_project`.

2. Set Up a Virtual Environment

Navigate to the project folder and create a virtual environment:

```bash
```

```
cd customer_churn_project
python -m venv venv
```

Activate the environment:

- On Windows:

```bash
```

```
venv\Scripts\activate
```

- ## On macOS/Linux:

```bash
bash
```

```
source venv/bin/activate
```

3. Install Libraries

Once the environment is activated, install the necessary libraries for this project:

```bash
bash
```

```
pip install scikit-learn pandas numpy matplotlib
seaborn jupyter
```

4. Create a Jupyter Notebook

Open Jupyter and start a new notebook inside the project folder:

```bash
bash
```

```
jupyter notebook
```

Create a new notebook called `customer_churn_analysis.ipynb` and start writing Python code. You can now import your data, clean it, explore it visually, and build your machine learning model—all within the Jupyter notebook.

This setup provides a controlled and reproducible environment where you can focus on writing code, analyzing data, and experimenting with machine learning models.

Summary

In this chapter, you:

- **Learned** why Python is the go-to language for machine learning, thanks to its simplicity, flexibility, and rich ecosystem.
- **Set up your Python environment** by installing Python, creating a virtual environment, and installing essential machine learning libraries.
- **Got introduced to Jupyter notebooks**, which are invaluable tools for interactive coding, documentation, and visualization.
- **Walked through a real-world example** of setting up an environment for a customer churn prediction project, which will help you understand how to structure and organize your machine learning work in Python.

With your environment set up and ready to go, you're now prepared to dive deeper into the world of machine learning using Python and Scikit-learn!

Chapter 2: Understanding Machine Learning: Basics and Terminology

What is Machine Learning and How Does It Differ from Traditional Programming?

Machine Learning (ML) is a subset of artificial intelligence (AI) that focuses on building systems capable of learning from data to make decisions, predictions, and improvements without being explicitly programmed. Instead of following fixed instructions written by a programmer, machine learning algorithms analyze patterns in data and "learn" how to perform tasks by training on large datasets.

In **traditional programming**, the process typically involves writing explicit instructions to solve a problem. For example, if you wanted a program to sort a list of numbers, you'd provide a specific algorithm like QuickSort or MergeSort and tell the computer exactly how to perform the sorting step by step.

However, in **machine learning**, the process is fundamentally different:

- **No explicit rules**: Rather than manually coding rules for specific problems, you provide a large amount of data, and the system learns the underlying patterns or relationships in the data on its own.

- **Learning from experience**: The algorithm improves its performance over time by being exposed to more data, adjusting its model to make more accurate predictions or decisions.
- **Generalization**: Machine learning models generalize the knowledge from the training data and apply it to new, unseen data.

For example, in a traditional program, if you wanted to identify whether an email was spam, you would manually write rules to detect spam-like content. In machine learning, you would feed the algorithm thousands of labeled emails (spam or not spam) and let it learn to recognize patterns that differentiate spam from non-spam emails.

Machine learning allows for automation of decision-making tasks that were previously too complex or time-consuming to program by hand.

Types of Machine Learning: Supervised, Unsupervised, and Reinforcement Learning

Machine learning can be broadly categorized into three main types, each with its own approach to learning and problem-solving:

1. **Supervised Learning**

- o **Definition**: In supervised learning, the algorithm learns from a labeled dataset, which means that the input data is accompanied by corresponding target labels (the "correct answers"). The model's goal is to learn a mapping from input features (data) to the target labels.
- o **How It Works**: The algorithm is trained using input-output pairs. After training, the model can make predictions on new, unseen data based on the patterns it has learned from the labeled training data.
- o **Common Algorithms**: Linear regression, logistic regression, decision trees, support vector machines, k-nearest neighbors, etc.
- o **Real-world Example**: Predicting house prices based on historical data (features like size, number of bedrooms, and location) is a supervised learning task. The target is the house price, and the model learns the relationship between features and price.

2. **Unsupervised Learning**
   - o **Definition**: In unsupervised learning, the algorithm works with unlabeled data, meaning there are no explicit target labels for the model

to learn from. The goal is to find underlying structure or patterns within the data.

- **How It Works**: The algorithm tries to identify inherent structures such as clusters, associations, or distributions in the data. It often involves grouping similar data points or reducing the data's dimensionality.
- **Common Algorithms**: K-means clustering, hierarchical clustering, principal component analysis (PCA), anomaly detection, etc.
- **Real-world Example**: In customer segmentation, unsupervised learning algorithms like k-means clustering can group customers based on similar behavior (e.g., spending habits, product preferences) without prior knowledge of the categories.

3. **Reinforcement Learning**
   - **Definition**: Reinforcement learning (RL) is inspired by behavioral psychology and focuses on how agents should take actions in an environment to maximize a cumulative reward. Unlike supervised learning, RL doesn't rely on labeled data. Instead, an agent learns through interactions with an environment, receiving

feedback (rewards or penalties) based on its actions.

- o **How It Works**: The agent explores the environment by taking actions and receiving feedback in the form of rewards or penalties. Over time, it learns to optimize its behavior to maximize long-term rewards.
- o **Common Algorithms**: Q-learning, deep Q-networks (DQN), policy gradient methods, etc.
- o **Real-world Example**: In a video game, an RL agent learns to play by taking actions (e.g., moving, jumping) and receiving feedback (e.g., points or losing health). Over time, the agent improves its strategy to achieve the highest possible score.

Real-World Example: Using Machine Learning for Product Recommendations

One of the most practical and impactful applications of machine learning in today's digital world is **product recommendation systems**. These systems help companies personalize the user experience by suggesting products or services based on a user's behavior and preferences. This is widely seen in e-commerce platforms like Amazon, Netflix, and Spotify, where the goal is to predict what a user will be interested in next.

Let's break down how machine learning can be used in product recommendations:

1. **Supervised Learning in Recommendation Systems**:
   - In some recommendation systems, supervised learning can be used to predict whether a customer will buy a product. For example, given a user's demographic information and past purchases, a model could predict whether they will buy a specific item. Techniques like logistic regression or decision trees could be used for binary classification tasks (e.g., predicting whether a user will purchase a product or not).

2. **Unsupervised Learning in Recommendation Systems**:
   - Unsupervised learning is often used for **collaborative filtering**, which is the basis of many recommendation systems. The system identifies patterns and similarities between users (or products) by grouping similar users together. For example:
     - **User-based collaborative filtering**: If User A and User B have similar

preferences, products liked by User A are recommended to User B.

- **Item-based collaborative filtering**: If users who liked Product X also liked Product Y, then Product Y is recommended to users who liked Product X.

- **K-means clustering** can be used to group customers based on their purchasing behavior, while **PCA** (Principal Component Analysis) might be used for reducing the dimensionality of complex customer datasets, making it easier to group similar users.

3. **Reinforcement Learning in Recommendation Systems**:
   - Reinforcement learning can be used to optimize the recommendation system over time by continually learning from user interactions. For example, an RL agent could dynamically adjust the products it recommends based on the reward feedback it receives when a user clicks on or purchases a product. The goal is to maximize the total user satisfaction (long-term reward) from product recommendations.

Example: Let's say you are building a product recommendation system for an online bookstore. Using machine learning:

- **Supervised learning** might predict whether a customer will purchase a book based on their previous interactions and demographic data.
- **Unsupervised learning** might group users into segments based on their book preferences and recommend books that are popular within those segments.
- **Reinforcement learning** might adjust the recommendations over time based on the customer's engagement with previous suggestions.

In , machine learning can significantly enhance product recommendation systems by analyzing vast amounts of user data, identifying patterns, and delivering personalized suggestions that improve user experience and drive business success.

Key Takeaways:

- Machine learning is a method of enabling systems to learn from data, without explicit programming.
- The three main types of machine learning are **supervised**, **unsupervised**, and **reinforcement learning**, each suited for different types of problems.
- Real-world applications, such as product recommendation systems, demonstrate how machine

learning can provide personalized experiences by analyzing data patterns and continuously improving over time.

In the next chapter, we will explore the **essential Python libraries** used for machine learning, starting with NumPy, pandas, and Scikit-learn, and learn how to implement machine learning models effectively in Python.

Chapter 3: Python for Data Science and Machine Learning

Essential Python Libraries for Machine Learning

Python is known for its extensive ecosystem of libraries that make data manipulation, analysis, and machine learning tasks easier. In this chapter, we'll explore the core libraries used in data science and machine learning, which are essential for handling data and building models.

1. NumPy: Numerical Computing

NumPy (Numerical Python) is the foundation of numerical computing in Python. It provides efficient tools for working with arrays, matrices, and numerical operations, which are vital for data manipulation in machine learning tasks.

- **Core Features**:
    - **N-dimensional arrays**: NumPy introduces the `ndarray`, which is a powerful n-dimensional array object for storing and manipulating data efficiently.
    - **Mathematical functions**: It provides a wide array of functions for performing operations like addition, subtraction, multiplication, trigonometric functions, and more, directly on arrays.

- o **Random number generation**: NumPy has functions to generate random numbers from different distributions, which is useful for tasks like data augmentation and initialization in machine learning.

- **Example**:

```python
import numpy as np
data = np.array([1, 2, 3, 4])
mean_value = np.mean(data)
print(f"Mean Value: {mean_value}")
```

2. pandas: Data Manipulation and Analysis

Pandas is a powerful library for data manipulation and analysis. It provides two essential data structures: **DataFrame** and **Series**, both of which are ideal for handling structured data.

- **Core Features**:
  - o **DataFrames**: A DataFrame is a two-dimensional, labeled data structure, akin to a spreadsheet or SQL table, where rows and columns represent data and labels.
  - o **Data manipulation**: You can clean, filter, and transform data using functions like `filter()`, `groupby()`, `merge()`, `drop()`, etc.

33

- o **Handling missing data**: pandas provides methods like `fillna()`, `dropna()`, and `isna()` for handling missing values.
- **Example**:

```python
import pandas as pd
data = {'Price': [50000, 60000, 55000], 'Size':
[1500, 1800, 1600]}
df = pd.DataFrame(data)
print(df)
```

3. Matplotlib: Data Visualization

Matplotlib is one of the most widely used libraries for creating static, animated, and interactive visualizations in Python. It provides a wide range of plotting tools to help you visualize datasets and the results of your machine learning models.

- **Core Features**:
  - o **Basic plotting**: Creating line plots, bar charts, histograms, scatter plots, and more.
  - o **Customization**: You can customize plots with labels, titles, colors, and legends.
  - o **Integration**: Works seamlessly with NumPy arrays and pandas DataFrames.
- **Example**:

```python
python

import matplotlib.pyplot as plt
x = [1, 2, 3, 4]
y = [2, 4, 6, 8]
plt.plot(x, y)
plt.xlabel('X Axis')
plt.ylabel('Y Axis')
plt.title('Simple Line Plot')
plt.show()
```

4. Seaborn: Advanced Visualization

Seaborn builds on Matplotlib and provides a higher-level interface for creating more aesthetically pleasing and complex visualizations. It integrates closely with pandas DataFrames and simplifies the process of plotting more sophisticated graphs.

- **Core Features**:
    - **Statistical plots**: Seaborn is excellent for visualizing statistical relationships in data, such as distributions, correlations, and trends.
    - **Heatmaps, pair plots, violin plots**: It offers high-level functions like `heatmap()`, `pairplot()`, and `violinplot()` that make it easier to visualize complex data relationships.
- **Example**:

```python
python
```

```
import seaborn as sns
import matplotlib.pyplot as plt
data = sns.load_dataset('iris')
sns.pairplot(data)
plt.show()
```

Introduction to Scikit-learn for Machine Learning

Scikit-learn is the most popular library for building machine learning models in Python. It provides a wide range of tools for data preprocessing, classification, regression, clustering, and model evaluation.

Core Features:

- **Preprocessing**: Scikit-learn includes utilities for scaling, encoding, and transforming data.
- **Supervised learning**: It includes popular supervised algorithms such as linear regression, logistic regression, decision trees, support vector machines, and more.
- **Unsupervised learning**: It also supports unsupervised algorithms like k-means clustering, DBSCAN, and PCA (Principal Component Analysis).
- **Model evaluation**: Scikit-learn includes tools for splitting datasets into training and testing sets,

performing cross-validation, and calculating model metrics like accuracy, precision, recall, and more.

Example:

In this example, we'll use Scikit-learn to perform a basic machine learning task—predicting housing prices using a linear regression model.

python

```
from sklearn.model_selection import train_test_split
from sklearn.linear_model import LinearRegression
from sklearn.metrics import mean_squared_error
import pandas as pd

# Load dataset
data = pd.read_csv('housing_data.csv')    # Example
dataset

# Preprocess data (for simplicity, we assume the
dataset is clean)
X = data[['Size', 'Bedrooms', 'Age']]  # Features
y = data['Price']  # Target variable

# Split data into training and testing sets
X_train,     X_test,     y_train,     y_test     =
train_test_split(X,        y,        test_size=0.2,
random_state=42)

# Initialize and train the model
```

```
model = LinearRegression()
model.fit(X_train, y_train)

# Make predictions
y_pred = model.predict(X_test)

# Evaluate model
mse = mean_squared_error(y_test, y_pred)
print(f'Mean Squared Error: {mse}')
```

Real-World Example: Data Preprocessing for a Real Estate Price Prediction Model

In this real-world example, we walk through the essential steps of preparing a dataset for machine learning. We will use **pandas** for data manipulation, **NumPy** for numerical operations, **Scikit-learn** for modeling, and **Matplotlib/Seaborn** for visualizing the data.

Steps for Data Preprocessing:

1. **Loading the Data**: First, we load the dataset containing information about real estate properties.

   ```python
   python
   ```

   ```python
   data = pd.read_csv('real_estate_data.csv')
   ```

2. **Handling Missing Data**: We check for missing values and decide whether to fill them with a default value (e.g., median) or drop rows.

python

```
data.fillna(data.median(), inplace=True)
```

3. **Feature Selection**: We select relevant features such as the size of the house, number of rooms, and location.

python

```
X = data[['Size', 'Bedrooms', 'Location']]
y = data['Price']
```

4. **Encoding Categorical Data**: For categorical variables like Location, we convert them into numerical representations using one-hot encoding.

python

```
X = pd.get_dummies(X, columns=['Location'])
```

5. **Scaling the Data**: We scale the numerical features to ensure that larger values (e.g., house size) don't dominate the learning process.

python

```
from        sklearn.preprocessing        import
StandardScaler
scaler = StandardScaler()
X_scaled = scaler.fit_transform(X)
```

6. **Splitting Data**: We divide the data into training and testing sets.

python

```
X_train,    X_test,    y_train,    y_test    =
train_test_split(X_scaled,    y,    test_size=0.2,
random_state=42)
```

7. **Model Training and Evaluation**: Using Scikit-learn, we train a linear regression model and evaluate its performance.

python

```
model = LinearRegression()
model.fit(X_train, y_train)
y_pred = model.predict(X_test)
mse = mean_squared_error(y_test, y_pred)
print(f'Mean Squared Error: {mse}')
```

This process of loading, cleaning, and transforming data is a critical part of the machine learning pipeline and is essential for building accurate models.

In this chapter, you learned about the essential libraries in Python for machine learning, how to preprocess data, and how to set up a basic model with Scikit-learn. By mastering these libraries, you can handle and manipulate real-world datasets to build effective machine learning models.

Chapter 4: Setting Up Scikit-Learn: Your First Model

Installing and Setting Up Scikit-learn

Scikit-learn is one of the most popular and comprehensive machine learning libraries in Python, built on top of NumPy, SciPy, and matplotlib. It provides simple and efficient tools for data mining and data analysis. This chapter will guide you through the process of installing Scikit-learn and setting up your environment to start building machine learning models.

1. Installing Scikit-learn

To use Scikit-learn, you first need to install it along with its dependencies. The recommended way to install Scikit-learn is through **pip** or **conda**.

- **Installing with pip**: Open your terminal or command prompt and run the following command:

  bash

```
pip install scikit-learn
```

- **Installing with conda** (if you are using Anaconda):

  bash

```
conda install scikit-learn
```

Both methods will install Scikit-learn along with its dependencies, such as NumPy and SciPy.

2. Verifying Installation

Once installed, you can verify that Scikit-learn is working by running the following code in a Python script or Jupyter notebook:

```python
```

```python
import sklearn
print(sklearn.__version__)
```

This will print the version of Scikit-learn you have installed. If no error occurs, the installation was successful.

Understanding Scikit-learn's Workflow: Loading Data, Fitting Models, Making Predictions

Scikit-learn provides a simple and consistent interface for working with machine learning models. The general workflow in Scikit-learn consists of the following key steps:

1. **Loading Data**: Loading or creating a dataset for training the model.
2. **Fitting the Model**: Training a machine learning model by applying it to the training data.
3. **Making Predictions**: Using the trained model to make predictions on new, unseen data.

4. **Evaluating the Model**: Assessing the performance of the model using various metrics.

5. **Improving the Model**: Tuning the model's hyperparameters and experimenting with different algorithms to improve performance.

1. Loading Data

In Scikit-learn, datasets are typically represented as NumPy arrays (for both input features and target labels). Many common datasets, such as the **Iris** dataset, **Boston housing** dataset, and others, are included with Scikit-learn, making it easy to get started.

For custom datasets (e.g., CSV files), you can use **pandas** to load the data and then convert it to the proper format for Scikit-learn.

Here's how to load a built-in dataset:

python

```python
from sklearn.datasets import load_boston
# Load the Boston housing dataset
data = load_boston()
X = data.data   # Features (input data)
y = data.target   # Labels (target data)
```

For a custom dataset, you would load it with pandas:

python

```python
import pandas as pd
data = pd.read_csv('your_data.csv')
```

```
X = data.drop(columns=['target'])
y = data['target']
```

2. Fitting the Model

Once the data is loaded, the next step is to select and apply a machine learning algorithm to fit the model. In Scikit-learn, this is typically done using the `fit()` method.

For example, for **linear regression**, Scikit-learn provides a simple implementation:

python

```
from sklearn.linear_model import LinearRegression
# Initialize the model
model = LinearRegression()
# Fit the model to the data
model.fit(X, y)
```

The `fit()` method adjusts the model's parameters based on the training data. In this case, it will compute the best-fitting line for predicting house prices based on the provided features.

3. Making Predictions

Once the model is trained, you can use it to make predictions on new data. This is done using the `predict()` method. For instance, to predict house prices on a new set of data:

python

```
# Assume X_new is a new dataset you want to predict
```

```
X_new = [[2500, 3, 2]]   # Example: 2500 sq ft, 3
bedrooms, 2 bathrooms
predictions = model.predict(X_new)
print(predictions)
```

The `predict()` method will return the predicted price for the house with the given features (e.g., size, number of bedrooms, etc.).

4. Evaluating the Model

After making predictions, it's crucial to assess the performance of the model. Scikit-learn provides various metrics to evaluate regression models, including **mean squared error (MSE), r-squared**, and more.

For example:

```python
from sklearn.metrics import mean_squared_error,
r2_score
y_pred = model.predict(X)
mse = mean_squared_error(y, y_pred)
r2 = r2_score(y, y_pred)
print(f'Mean Squared Error: {mse}')
print(f'R-squared: {r2}')
```

- **Mean Squared Error (MSE)**: This metric calculates the average of the squared differences between the actual and predicted values. A lower MSE indicates a better model.

- **R-squared**: This statistic measures how well the model's predictions match the actual data. A value closer to 1 indicates a better fit.

Real-World Example: Building a Simple Linear Regression Model to Predict House Prices

Let's walk through a real-world example where we build a simple linear regression model to predict house prices based on the size of the house (in square feet). We'll use Scikit-learn to implement this step by step.

1. **Step 1: Import Libraries and Load Data**

Let's create a dataset with the features (house size) and the target (house price):

python

```
import numpy as np
import pandas as pd
from sklearn.linear_model import LinearRegression
from sklearn.metrics import mean_squared_error,
r2_score
import matplotlib.pyplot as plt

# Example dataset: House size (in sq ft) and price
(in dollars)
```

```python
data = {'Size': [1500, 1800, 2400, 3000, 3500],
        'Price': [400000, 450000, 500000, 550000,
600000]}
df = pd.DataFrame(data)

# Feature (X) and target (y)
X = df[['Size']]  # House size as the feature
y = df['Price']  # House price as the target
```

2. Step 2: Initialize and Fit the Model

python

```python
# Create the model instance
model = LinearRegression()

# Fit the model
model.fit(X, y)
```

3. Step 3: Make Predictions

python

```python
# Predict prices using the trained model
y_pred = model.predict(X)
print(f"Predicted prices: {y_pred}")
```

4. Step 4: Evaluate the Model

python

```
# Calculate MSE and R-squared
mse = mean_squared_error(y, y_pred)
r2 = r2_score(y, y_pred)

print(f'Mean Squared Error: {mse}')
print(f'R-squared: {r2}')
```

5. **Step 5: Visualize the Results** To visualize the fitted line:

python

```
plt.scatter(X, y, color='blue')  # Actual data points
plt.plot(X, y_pred, color='red')  # Predicted line
plt.title('House Price Prediction')
plt.xlabel('Size (sq ft)')
plt.ylabel('Price (USD)')
plt.show()
```

In this example, we've used a simple linear regression model to predict house prices based on their sizes. By evaluating the performance with metrics like MSE and R-squared, we can gauge how well the model fits the data.

Chapter 5: Data Importing and Exploration with Python

Data preprocessing is one of the most critical steps in any data science or machine learning project. Before you can apply machine learning models, it's essential to understand and prepare your data. This chapter will guide you through the process of importing data from various sources, performing initial explorations, and understanding key data characteristics using Python libraries such as **pandas**.

1. Importing Data from CSV, Excel, and Databases Using pandas

pandas is the go-to Python library for working with structured data. It provides easy-to-use data structures (such as `DataFrame`) and a wide variety of functions for importing, cleaning, and manipulating data. We'll explore how to import data from three common sources: **CSV files**, **Excel files**, and **databases**.

1.1 Importing Data from CSV Files

CSV (Comma Separated Values) is one of the most common data formats for storing and sharing data. You can easily import CSV files into Python using the `pandas` function `read_csv()`.

Example:

```python
```

```
import pandas as pd
# Importing data from a CSV file
data = pd.read_csv('customer_data.csv')
# Display the first few rows of the data
print(data.head())
```

In this example, `read_csv()` reads the CSV file and loads it into a **DataFrame**, a two-dimensional data structure in pandas that is ideal for manipulating and analyzing data.

1.2 Importing Data from Excel Files

Many datasets are stored in Excel format, particularly when they come from business or finance-related contexts. pandas provides the `read_excel()` function to load Excel files.

Example:

```
python
```

```
# Importing data from an Excel file
data        =        pd.read_excel('customer_data.xlsx',
sheet_name='Sheet1')
# Display the first few rows of the data
print(data.head())
```

Note that the `sheet_name` parameter is used to specify which sheet within the Excel file to import.

1.3 Importing Data from Databases

For more complex datasets, especially in real-world applications, data may reside in relational databases (like MySQL, PostgreSQL, or SQLite). pandas allows you to connect to a database using SQL queries to import the data into Python.

Example (using SQLite):

```python
```

```python
import sqlite3
import pandas as pd
# Connect to SQLite database
conn = sqlite3.connect('customer_data.db')
# Import data from the database
data = pd.read_sql_query("SELECT * FROM customers",
conn)
# Display the first few rows of the data
print(data.head())
```

The `read_sql_query()` function executes the SQL query and loads the result directly into a pandas DataFrame.

---

2. Exploring Data with pandas: Understanding Data Types, Missing Values, and Descriptive Statistics

Once the data is loaded into a pandas DataFrame, the next step is to explore it. This allows you to understand its structure, identify potential issues (like missing data or incorrect data types), and get an overview of key characteristics.

2.1 Understanding Data Types

In any dataset, it's important to know the types of data you're working with. pandas automatically infers the data type for each column, but you can check the data types explicitly using the `dtypes` attribute.

Example:

```python
python
```

```python
# Check the data types of each column
print(data.dtypes)
```

This will output the data type for each column (e.g., `int64`, `float64`, `object`, etc.). If the types are incorrect (e.g., numeric data is stored as text), you may need to convert columns to the appropriate types using methods like `astype()`.

Example:

```python
python
```

```python
# Convert a column to numeric
data['Age']          =          pd.to_numeric(data['Age'],
errors='coerce')
```

The `errors='coerce'` argument ensures that invalid parsing errors are replaced with `NaN`.

2.2 Handling Missing Values

In real-world datasets, missing values are common. These missing values can be represented as `NaN` (Not a Number) or sometimes as empty strings or special markers (e.g., None or NULL). You can identify and handle missing values using various pandas functions.

- **Checking for Missing Values**: To check for missing values in your DataFrame, use the isna() method, which returns a DataFrame of the same shape, with True for missing values and False for non-missing values.

```python
# Check for missing values
print(data.isna().sum())
```

This will show you the count of missing values per column.

- **Handling Missing Values**: You can handle missing values by either filling them with a specific value or dropping them entirely.
  - **Filling missing values**: Use fillna() to replace missing values with a constant or a statistical value (e.g., mean or median).

```python
data['Age']                        =
data['Age'].fillna(data['Age'].mean())
```

  - **Dropping missing values**: Use dropna() to remove rows or columns with missing values.

```python
python

data = data.dropna()
```

2.3 Descriptive Statistics

Descriptive statistics help you understand the basic features of the data. Pandas makes it easy to compute common statistical measures such as mean, median, standard deviation, and more.

- **Basic Summary**: The `describe()` method provides a summary of statistics for numerical columns.

```python
python

print(data.describe())
```

This will include metrics like the mean, standard deviation, minimum, and maximum for each numerical column in the DataFrame.

- **Additional Statistics**: You can also calculate specific statistics like the mode (most frequent value) using `mode()` and the variance using `var()`.

```python
python

mode_value = data['Age'].mode()
print(f"Mode of Age: {mode_value}")
```

- **Exploring Categorical Data**: For categorical variables (like gender or product categories), you can use the `value_counts()` method to see how many unique values exist and their frequencies.

```python
python

print(data['Gender'].value_counts())
```

3. Real-World Example: Importing and Exploring a Dataset of Customer Demographics

In this section, we'll go through a real-world example where we import and explore a customer demographic dataset.

- **Dataset**: Assume we have a dataset named `customer_demographics.csv`, which contains the following columns:
  - `CustomerID`: Unique identifier for each customer.
  - `Age`: Age of the customer.
  - `Gender`: Gender of the customer (Male/Female).
  - `AnnualIncome`: Customer's annual income.
  - `PurchaseHistory`: Number of products purchased in the past year.
- **Steps**:

1. Import the dataset:

```python
data = pd.read_csv('customer_demographics.csv')
```

2. Check the first few rows of the dataset to ensure it loaded correctly:

```python
print(data.head())
```

3. Check for missing values:

```python
print(data.isna().sum())
```

4. Convert the `Age` column to numeric if necessary:

```python
data['Age'] = pd.to_numeric(data['Age'], errors='coerce')
```

5. Fill missing values for `Age` with the mean:

```python
```

```
data['Age']                              =
data['Age'].fillna(data['Age'].mean())
```

6.   Get a summary of descriptive statistics:

```python
```

```
print(data.describe())
```

7.   Examine the distribution of categorical data (Gender):

```python
```

```
print(data['Gender'].value_counts())
```

By the end of this chapter, you will have learned how to import data from different sources (CSV, Excel, databases), explore the dataset to understand its structure and characteristics, handle missing data, and perform basic statistical analysis on your data. These steps form the foundation for successful machine learning and data analysis.

Chapter 6: Data Cleaning: Handling Missing Values and Outliers

Data cleaning is one of the most time-consuming yet crucial aspects of a data science project. Before you can proceed with any analysis or modeling, it's essential to clean the data by handling missing values, duplicates, and outliers. In this chapter, we will explore various techniques to clean your dataset using **pandas**, ensuring that the data is in the right format for analysis or machine learning.

1. Techniques for Handling Missing Values

Missing data is one of the most common issues you'll encounter during data preprocessing. How you handle missing values depends on the context of your data and the problem you are trying to solve.

1.1 Identifying Missing Values

In **pandas**, missing values are typically represented as NaN (Not a Number). To identify missing values, you can use the isnull() function, which returns a DataFrame of Boolean values (True for missing, False for non-missing).

Example:

```python
python
```

```
import pandas as pd
# Check for missing values in the DataFrame
missing_values = data.isnull()
print(missing_values.sum())    # Count  of  missing
values per column
```

This will give you the number of missing values in each column of your dataset.

1.2 Removing Rows or Columns with Missing Values

If you have rows or columns with missing values, you can either remove them or impute them (fill in with appropriate values). To drop rows with missing values, use the dropna() function:

python

```
# Drop rows with any missing values
data_cleaned = data.dropna()
```

If you want to drop columns with missing values, you can specify the axis:

python

```
# Drop columns with missing values
data_cleaned = data.dropna(axis=1)
```

1.3 Filling Missing Values (Imputation)

In many cases, removing data may not be ideal, especially when dealing with large datasets. Instead, you can fill missing values (impute) with various strategies like the mean, median, or mode of the column.

- **Filling with the mean** (useful for numerical columns):

python

```
data['Sales']                                    =
data['Sales'].fillna(data['Sales'].mean())
```

- **Filling with the median** (useful for skewed data):

python

```
data['Sales']                                    =
data['Sales'].fillna(data['Sales'].median())
```

- **Filling with the mode** (useful for categorical data):

python

```
data['Category']                                 =
data['Category'].fillna(data['Category'].mode()
[0])
```

- **Forward or backward filling**:

python

```
# Fill missing values with the previous row's
value
data['Sales']                                    =
data['Sales'].fillna(method='ffill')
```

1.4 Interpolation

For time-series data, interpolation can be a useful technique for filling missing values. pandas provides an `interpolate()` function that can estimate missing values based on surrounding data points.

```python
python
```

```python
# Interpolate missing values in a column
data['Sales'] = data['Sales'].interpolate()
```

---

2. Handling Duplicates

Duplicate entries can distort your analysis or model, leading to biased results. It's important to identify and remove duplicate rows from your dataset.

2.1 Identifying Duplicates

You can identify duplicate rows using the `duplicated()` function, which returns a Boolean Series indicating whether each row is a duplicate (excluding the first occurrence).

Example:

```python
python
```

```python
# Identify duplicate rows
duplicates = data.duplicated()
print(duplicates.sum())  # Count of duplicate rows
```

2.2 Removing Duplicates

To remove duplicate rows, you can use the `drop_duplicates()` function. By default, it keeps the first occurrence and removes the subsequent duplicates.

```python
python
```

```python
# Remove duplicate rows
data_cleaned = data.drop_duplicates()
```

If you want to keep the last occurrence instead, you can specify `keep='last'`:

```python
python
```

```python
# Keep the last occurrence of duplicates
data_cleaned = data.drop_duplicates(keep='last')
```

---

3. Handling Outliers

Outliers are extreme values that differ significantly from the rest of the data. They can skew statistical analyses and models, leading to inaccurate predictions. Identifying and handling outliers is crucial for data preprocessing.

3.1 Identifying Outliers

There are several methods to detect outliers, with the most common being:

- **Z-Score**: This method identifies outliers based on how many standard deviations a data point is away from the mean.

  A Z-score greater than 3 or less than -3 is often considered an outlier.

  python

  ```
  from scipy import stats
  z_scores = stats.zscore(data['Sales'])
  outliers = data[abs(z_scores) > 3]
  print(outliers)
  ```

- **IQR (Interquartile Range)**: The IQR method identifies outliers based on the spread of the middle 50% of the data. Any value below Q1 - 1.5 * IQR or above Q3 + 1.5 * IQR is considered an outlier.

  python

  ```
  Q1 = data['Sales'].quantile(0.25)
  Q3 = data['Sales'].quantile(0.75)
  IQR = Q3 - Q1
  lower_bound = Q1 - 1.5 * IQR
  upper_bound = Q3 + 1.5 * IQR
  outliers = data[(data['Sales'] < lower_bound) |
  (data['Sales'] > upper_bound)]
  print(outliers)
  ```

3.2 Handling Outliers

Once outliers are identified, you have several options for dealing with them:

- **Removing Outliers**: If you believe the outliers are data errors or irrelevant, you can remove them.

  python

  ```
  data_cleaned    =    data[(data['Sales']    >=
  lower_bound) & (data['Sales'] <= upper_bound)]
  ```

- **Transforming Data**: If outliers are a natural part of the data but need to be handled for modeling purposes, you can apply transformations like **log transformation** or **Box-Cox transformation** to reduce their impact.

  Example:

  python

  ```
  import numpy as np
  data['Sales']   =   np.log1p(data['Sales'])    #
  Apply log transformation
  ```

- **Imputing Outliers**: In some cases, you may want to replace outliers with more reasonable values, such as the median or mean.

```python
python

median_value = data['Sales'].median()
data['Sales']    =    np.where((data['Sales']    <
lower_bound)  |  (data['Sales']  >  upper_bound),
median_value, data['Sales'])
```

4. Real-World Example: Cleaning Sales Data for Analysis

Imagine you are tasked with analyzing sales data for an e-commerce company. The data consists of sales transactions over several months, including columns for Product ID, Sales Amount, Quantity Sold, and Customer Location. However, this dataset contains some issues:

- **Missing Values**: Some transactions have missing values for Sales Amount or Quantity Sold.
- **Duplicates**: Some transactions are repeated, possibly due to an error during data entry.
- **Outliers**: There are some unusually high sales amounts that don't seem realistic.

To clean this dataset:

1. **Handle Missing Values**: Impute missing sales amounts with the median or mean of the column, and remove rows with missing Quantity Sold if necessary.

66

2. **Remove Duplicates**: Drop duplicate transactions to ensure accurate analysis.
3. **Handle Outliers**: Identify outliers using the IQR method and either remove or transform them based on the business context.

Here's how you might apply these techniques:

python

```python
# Impute missing sales data
data['Sales        Amount']        =        data['Sales
Amount'].fillna(data['Sales Amount'].median())

# Remove duplicate transactions
data_cleaned = data.drop_duplicates()

# Remove outliers in Sales Amount
Q1 = data_cleaned['Sales Amount'].quantile(0.25)
Q3 = data_cleaned['Sales Amount'].quantile(0.75)
IQR = Q3 - Q1
lower_bound = Q1 - 1.5 * IQR
upper_bound = Q3 + 1.5 * IQR
data_cleaned    =    data_cleaned[(data_cleaned['Sales
Amount']   >=   lower_bound)   &   (data_cleaned['Sales
Amount'] <= upper_bound)]

print(data_cleaned.head())
```

By the end of this chapter, you'll have a solid understanding of how to clean and prepare your data for further analysis or machine learning tasks.

Chapter 7: Feature Engineering: Transforming Data for ML Models

Feature engineering is a key step in the machine learning pipeline. It involves creating new features from raw data, transforming existing features into more useful formats, and preparing the dataset in such a way that it enhances the performance of machine learning models. In this chapter, we'll discuss various techniques for feature engineering, including encoding categorical variables, scaling numerical data, and creating new features based on domain knowledge. We'll also walk through a real-world example of feature engineering for **customer churn prediction**.

1. Creating New Features from Existing Data

Creating new features from existing data is an essential part of feature engineering. By combining or transforming current features, you can unlock hidden patterns that may be important for machine learning models. There are a few common techniques for creating new features:

1.1 Binning (Discretization)

Sometimes, continuous numerical features can be converted into categorical ones by grouping them into bins or intervals. This can be useful when there is no clear relationship between the original feature and the target, but the intervals might provide useful insights.

Example:

python

```
# Binning the 'age' column into 3 age groups:
'Young', 'Middle-Aged', 'Old'
bins = [0, 25, 50, 100]
labels = ['Young', 'Middle-Aged', 'Old']
data['AgeGroup'] = pd.cut(data['Age'], bins=bins,
labels=labels)
```

1.2 Creating Interaction Features

Sometimes, the relationship between two features is more important than the features themselves. Interaction features capture such relationships by combining two or more features.

Example:

python

```
# Creating an interaction feature between 'Income'
and 'Age'
data['Income_Age_Interaction'] = data['Income'] *
data['Age']
```

1.3 Feature Extraction from Date/Time

In datasets that include date or time columns, you can extract useful features such as day of the week, month, quarter, or even the time since an event occurred.

Example:

```python
python

# Extracting features from a 'SignupDate' column
data['SignupYear']                              =
pd.to_datetime(data['SignupDate']).dt.year
data['SignupMonth']                             =
pd.to_datetime(data['SignupDate']).dt.month
data['SignupDayOfWeek']                         =
pd.to_datetime(data['SignupDate']).dt.dayofweek
```

2. Encoding Categorical Variables

Many machine learning algorithms require input features to be numerical. Therefore, it is necessary to encode categorical variables into numeric formats. There are a few common techniques for encoding categorical data:

2.1 Label Encoding

Label encoding transforms each category into a unique integer. This method is useful when the categorical variable has a natural order (ordinal data).

Example:

```python
python

from sklearn.preprocessing import LabelEncoder
# Encoding the 'Gender' column
label_encoder = LabelEncoder()
```

```
data['Gender_encoded']                              =
label_encoder.fit_transform(data['Gender'])
```

2.2 One-Hot Encoding

One-hot encoding creates a binary column for each category, where a 1 indicates the presence of that category and a 0 indicates its absence. This method is ideal for nominal data where there is no inherent order.

Example:

python

```
# One-hot encoding the 'Category' column
data   =   pd.get_dummies(data,   columns=['Category'],
drop_first=True)
```

In this example, the `drop_first=True` argument avoids multicollinearity by removing one category (it serves as a baseline).

2.3 Target Encoding

Target encoding replaces categorical labels with the mean of the target variable for each category. This method is often useful for high-cardinality features.

Example:

python

```
# Target encoding for 'ProductType' based on 'Churn'
target variable
```

```
data['ProductType_encoded']                          =
data.groupby('ProductType')['Churn'].transform('mean'
)
```

---

3. Scaling Numerical Data

Many machine learning algorithms, such as **linear regression**, **SVMs**, and **k-nearest neighbors**, perform better when the numerical features are on a similar scale. Scaling ensures that each feature contributes equally to the model's learning process.

3.1 Standardization (Z-score Normalization)

Standardization transforms features by removing the mean and scaling to unit variance (z-scores). This is useful when the data follows a Gaussian distribution.

Example:

python

```
from sklearn.preprocessing import StandardScaler
# Standardizing 'Income' and 'Age' columns
scaler = StandardScaler()
data[['Income',                    'Age']]            =
scaler.fit_transform(data[['Income', 'Age']])
```

3.2 Min-Max Scaling

Min-max scaling rescales the data to a fixed range, typically [0, 1]. This method is often used when the data is not normally distributed or when you want to bound the data to a specific range.

Example:

python

```
from sklearn.preprocessing import MinMaxScaler
# Rescaling 'Income' and 'Age' columns to [0, 1]
scaler = MinMaxScaler()
data[['Income',                 'Age']]                    =
scaler.fit_transform(data[['Income', 'Age']])
```

3.3 Robust Scaling

Robust scaling uses the median and the interquartile range (IQR) for scaling. It is particularly useful when your dataset contains outliers.

Example:

python

```
from sklearn.preprocessing import RobustScaler
# Scaling 'Income' and 'Age' with robust scaling
scaler = RobustScaler()
data[['Income',                 'Age']]                    =
scaler.fit_transform(data[['Income', 'Age']])
```

---

4. Real-World Example: Feature Engineering for Customer Churn Prediction

Let's apply these feature engineering techniques in a real-world scenario. Suppose you're building a machine learning model to predict customer churn in a telecom company. The dataset includes features like `Age`, `Income`, `AccountType`, `SignupDate`, and `CustomerServiceCalls`.

4.1 Creating New Features

- **Customer Tenure**: Calculate the number of months since the customer signed up.

python

```
data['TenureMonths'] = (pd.to_datetime('today') -
pd.to_datetime(data['SignupDate'])).dt.days // 30
```

- **Interaction Feature**: Customer's `Income` and `TenureMonths` might interact in predicting churn, so we create an interaction term:

python

```
data['Income_Tenure_Interaction'] = data['Income'] *
data['TenureMonths']
```

4.2 Encoding Categorical Features

- **AccountType Encoding**: Convert `AccountType` (e.g., 'Basic', 'Premium', 'VIP') into numerical values using **one-hot encoding**:

python

```
data = pd.get_dummies(data, columns=['AccountType'],
drop_first=True)
```

4.3 Scaling Features

- **Income Scaling**: Since `Income` is a continuous feature, standardize it:

python

```
scaler = StandardScaler()
data['Income']                                    =
scaler.fit_transform(data[['Income']])
```

4.4 Handling Missing Values

Before fitting the model, ensure that all missing values are handled, as discussed earlier. For instance:

python

```
data['CustomerServiceCalls'].fillna(data['CustomerSer
viceCalls'].mode()[0], inplace=True)
```

5.

Feature engineering is a creative and iterative process. By transforming raw data into meaningful features, you can significantly enhance the performance of your machine learning models. The techniques outlined in this chapter, such as creating new features, encoding categorical variables, and scaling numerical data, are foundational skills in data preprocessing. The real-world example of **customer churn prediction** demonstrates how to apply these methods to prepare data for machine learning. With a solid understanding of feature engineering, you are well on your way to building more accurate and robust machine learning models.

Chapter 8: Splitting Data for Training and Testing

One of the key steps in building a machine learning model is to divide your dataset into two or more subsets: one for training the model and the other for testing or validating its performance. This practice ensures that your model is not overfitting to the training data and can generalize well to new, unseen data. In this chapter, we will cover the importance of splitting data, the techniques for splitting data effectively, and how to use Scikit-learn's `train_test_split` method. We'll also walk through a real-world example of splitting data for a **binary classification model**.

1. Why Split Data into Training and Testing Sets?

When building a machine learning model, you want to evaluate its ability to generalize beyond the data it was trained on. If you use the same dataset for both training and testing, there is a risk that the model will simply memorize the training data, leading to **overfitting**. Overfitting means the model performs well on the training data but poorly on new, unseen data.

By splitting your data into at least two sets—**training** and **testing**—you can:

- Train the model on one subset (the training set).

- Test its performance on another subset (the testing set) that it has never seen before. This helps to estimate how well the model will perform in real-world scenarios, where it encounters unseen data.

1.1 Train-Validation-Test Split

In addition to the basic training and testing sets, some projects involve creating a **validation set**. This validation set is used to fine-tune hyperparameters and evaluate the model during training. This results in a three-way split:

- **Training Set**: Used to train the model.
- **Validation Set**: Used to tune model parameters (optional but highly recommended).
- **Test Set**: Used to evaluate the final model's performance after training.

However, in many cases, especially for simpler projects, a **train-test split** is sufficient.

2. How to Split Data into Training and Testing Sets

The general process of splitting data is as follows:

1. **Shuffle the Data**: Randomly shuffle the dataset to avoid any bias in the order of data.

2. **Split the Data**: Divide the data into training and testing subsets.
3. **Train the Model**: Train your model on the training set.
4. **Evaluate the Model**: Evaluate the model's performance on the testing set.

The **split ratio** (e.g., 80% for training and 20% for testing) can be adjusted depending on the size of the dataset and the specific requirements of the model. Common ratios are:

- **80-20 split**: 80% of data for training, 20% for testing.
- **70-30 split**: 70% of data for training, 30% for testing.
- **60-40 split**: 60% of data for training, 40% for testing (typically used for smaller datasets).

---

3. Using Scikit-learn's `train_test_split` Method

Scikit-learn provides a simple and efficient method for splitting your data: `train_test_split()`. This function randomly splits data into training and testing subsets. It is important to note that this function also allows you to shuffle the data before splitting, ensuring that the data is not ordered in any way that could introduce bias.

3.1 Syntax of `train_test_split`

The `train_test_split()` function splits arrays or matrices into random train and test subsets.

python

```
from sklearn.model_selection import train_test_split

# Split the data into training and testing sets (80%
training, 20% testing)
X_train,      X_test,      y_train,      y_test      =
train_test_split(X,          y,           test_size=0.2,
random_state=42)
```

- x: Feature set (input variables).
- y: Target variable (output or labels).
- `test_size`: Proportion of the data to be used as the test set (0.2 means 20% for testing, 80% for training).
- `random_state`: Ensures reproducibility of the split. If you use the same `random_state`, you'll get the same split each time you run the code.

3.2 Example: Splitting Data for Binary Classification

Let's consider a dataset where we are trying to predict customer churn (binary classification: churn or no churn). The dataset consists of features such as **age, income, account type**, etc., and a target variable Churn (where 1 indicates churn and 0 indicates no churn).

python

```python
import pandas as pd
from sklearn.model_selection import train_test_split

# Load the dataset
data = pd.read_csv('customer_churn.csv')

# Features and target
X = data[['Age', 'Income', 'AccountType']]  # Feature set
y = data['Churn']  # Target variable

# Split the data into training and testing sets (80%
training, 20% testing)
X_train,     X_test,     y_train,     y_test     =
train_test_split(X,          y,          test_size=0.2,
random_state=42)

# Display the shape of the splits
print(f'Training   set:   {X_train.shape[0]}   samples,
Testing set: {X_test.shape[0]} samples')
```

In this example:

- The `train_test_split()` function divides the dataset into training and testing sets.
- The `test_size=0.2` parameter ensures that 20% of the data will be used for testing, and 80% will be used for training.

- The `random_state=42` ensures that every time we run this code, we'll get the same split.

3.3 Stratified Sampling (Optional)

For certain datasets, especially in **imbalanced classes** (like churn prediction where the target classes are highly imbalanced), it's a good idea to maintain the same distribution of classes in both the training and testing sets. Scikit-learn's `train_test_split` allows for **stratified sampling**, which ensures that the proportion of each class is the same in both splits.

python

```
# Stratified split based on the target variable
'Churn'
X_train,    X_test,    y_train,    y_test    =
train_test_split(X,   y,   test_size=0.2,   stratify=y,
random_state=42)
```

In this example, the `stratify=y` argument ensures that the class distribution of `y` is preserved in both the training and testing sets.

---

4. *Real-World Example: Splitting Data for Binary Classification Model*

Let's say we're building a binary classification model to predict whether a customer will churn based on their demographic and account data. In the previous code example, we used

83

`train_test_split` to divide the dataset into training and testing sets, allowing us to evaluate the model's performance effectively.

After splitting the data, we can proceed to:

- **Train the model** on the training data (e.g., using Logistic Regression, Decision Trees, etc.).
- **Evaluate the model** on the testing data to see how well it generalizes to unseen examples.

Example:

python

```
from sklearn.linear_model import LogisticRegression
from sklearn.metrics import accuracy_score,
confusion_matrix

# Initialize the model
model = LogisticRegression()

# Train the model on the training data
model.fit(X_train, y_train)

# Predict on the testing data
y_pred = model.predict(X_test)

# Evaluate the model's performance
print(f'Accuracy: {accuracy_score(y_test,
y_pred):.2f}')
```

```
print(f'Confusion    Matrix:\n{confusion_matrix(y_test,
y_pred)}')
```

Summary

In this chapter, we:

- Explored the importance of splitting data into **training** and **testing** sets to prevent overfitting and ensure generalizability.
- Learned how to use Scikit-learn's `train_test_split` function to split data effectively.
- Walked through an example of **binary classification** where we predicted customer churn. By splitting your data correctly, you ensure that your model is evaluated on unseen data, providing a realistic estimate of its performance when deployed in real-world applications.

Chapter 9: Introduction to Supervised Learning

Supervised learning is one of the most widely used approaches in machine learning. It involves training a model on a labeled dataset, where both the input data and the corresponding output (or labels) are provided. The goal of supervised learning is to learn the relationship between the input features and the output labels so that the model can make accurate predictions on unseen data. In this chapter, we will explore the key concepts of supervised learning, including how it works, its types, and its applications. We will also walk through a real-world example of using supervised learning for **predicting loan default**.

---

1. What is Supervised Learning?

In supervised learning, we use labeled data to train a machine learning model. This means that for every input sample, we also know the correct output or label. The model learns the mapping between the inputs (features) and the labels through a training process. Once trained, the model can be used to predict the labels for new, unseen data.

For example:

- **Input**: Data about a borrower, such as their credit score, income, loan amount, etc.
- **Output (Label)**: Whether the borrower defaulted on the loan or not (binary classification).

Supervised learning models are typically divided into two main categories based on the type of output:

1. **Classification**: The model predicts discrete labels (e.g., yes/no, spam/ham, or classifying animals into species).
2. **Regression**: The model predicts continuous values (e.g., house prices, temperature, stock prices).

2. The Supervised Learning Process

The supervised learning process generally follows these steps:

1. **Data Collection**: Collect labeled data for the task.
2. **Data Preprocessing**: Clean the data and transform it into a format suitable for the model (e.g., handling missing values, encoding categorical variables).
3. **Model Selection**: Choose an appropriate machine learning algorithm (e.g., linear regression, decision trees, random forests, support vector machines, etc.).

4. **Model Training**: Use the training data to train the model by fitting it to the data.

5. **Model Evaluation**: Evaluate the performance of the model on the testing data using various metrics like accuracy, precision, recall, F1-score (for classification), or mean squared error (for regression).

6. **Model Tuning**: Fine-tune the model by adjusting hyperparameters to improve its performance.

7. **Prediction**: Use the trained model to make predictions on new, unseen data.

---

3. Types of Supervised Learning

There are two primary types of supervised learning problems: **classification** and **regression**.

3.1 Classification

In classification tasks, the output variable (target) is a discrete class or category. The goal is to assign each input to one of these predefined classes. Common examples of classification tasks include:

- **Binary classification**: Predicting whether an event will happen or not (e.g., predicting if a customer will churn: yes or no).

- **Multiclass classification**: Assigning an input to one of several categories (e.g., predicting the type of fruit: apple, banana, or orange).

Common classification algorithms include:

- **Logistic Regression**
- **K-Nearest Neighbors (KNN)**
- **Decision Trees**
- **Random Forest**
- **Support Vector Machines (SVM)**

3.2 Regression

In regression tasks, the output variable is continuous. The goal is to predict a numerical value based on the input features. Common examples of regression tasks include:

- **Predicting house prices** based on features such as location, size, and age.
- **Predicting stock prices** based on historical data.

Common regression algorithms include:

- **Linear Regression**
- **Polynomial Regression**
- **Decision Trees (for Regression)**
- **Random Forest Regression**

- **Support Vector Regression (SVR)**

---

4. Real-World Example: Predicting Loan Default Using Supervised Learning

Let's consider a real-world example of using supervised learning to predict whether a borrower will default on a loan. This is a **binary classification** problem, where the two possible outputs are:

- **0 (No Default)**: The borrower will not default on the loan.
- **1 (Default)**: The borrower will default on the loan.

4.1 The Problem

We have a dataset containing various features about each borrower, such as:

- **Credit Score**: A numerical value that indicates the borrower's creditworthiness.
- **Income**: The borrower's monthly income.
- **Loan Amount**: The amount of loan requested.
- **Employment Status**: Whether the borrower is employed or self-employed.
- **Loan Term**: The length of time over which the loan will be repaid.

The target variable in this case is whether the borrower will default or not (i.e., 0 or 1).

4.2 Steps in Solving the Problem

1. **Data Collection**: Collect a dataset containing historical information on borrowers, including their features and whether they defaulted or not.

2. **Data Preprocessing**:
   o **Handle missing values**: Fill or drop missing data.
   o **Encode categorical variables**: For example, "Employment Status" may need to be encoded as numerical values.
   o **Feature scaling**: Standardize numerical features like "Income" and "Loan Amount" to bring them to a similar scale.

Example code:

python

```
from sklearn.preprocessing import StandardScaler
scaler = StandardScaler()
data[['Income', 'LoanAmount']] = scaler.fit_transform(data[['Income', 'LoanAmount']])
```

3. **Model Selection**: Choose a supervised learning algorithm. For this binary classification problem, we can use models like **Logistic Regression**, **Random Forest**, or **Support Vector Machines (SVM)**.

4. **Model Training**: Use the training data to fit the model. Example code using **Logistic Regression**:

python

```
from        sklearn.linear_model        import
LogisticRegression
model = LogisticRegression()
model.fit(X_train, y_train)
```

5. **Model Evaluation**: Evaluate the model's performance on the test set using metrics such as **accuracy**, **precision**, **recall**, and **F1-score**. Example code:

python

```
from   sklearn.metrics   import   accuracy_score,
classification_report
y_pred = model.predict(X_test)
print(accuracy_score(y_test, y_pred))
print(classification_report(y_test, y_pred))
```

6. **Model Tuning**: Adjust hyperparameters like regularization strength (for logistic regression) or the number of trees (for random forest) to improve model performance.

7. **Prediction**: Once the model is trained and evaluated, use it to make predictions for new borrowers.

5.

Supervised learning is an essential technique in machine learning, and it powers many real-world applications, from fraud detection to recommendation systems. By understanding the basics of supervised learning and its different types (classification and regression), you can approach a wide range of predictive tasks. In this chapter, we introduced the concepts of supervised learning and provided a detailed example of using it to predict loan defaults. By applying these techniques to real-world datasets, you can build powerful predictive models that solve complex problems and deliver actionable insights.

Chapter 10: Linear Regression: Predicting Continuous Values

Linear regression is one of the simplest and most commonly used algorithms in machine learning and statistics for predicting continuous values. It models the relationship between one or more input variables (also called features) and a continuous output variable. In this chapter, we will cover the steps to build and interpret a linear regression model, evaluate its performance using metrics like R^2 and Mean Squared Error (MSE), and walk through a real-world example of predicting **sales revenue** based on an **advertising budget**.

---

1. What is Linear Regression?

Linear regression is a statistical method used for modeling the relationship between a dependent variable (the output or target variable) and one or more independent variables (the input features). In simple linear regression, the relationship between the dependent variable YYY and the independent variable XXX is modeled as a straight line, represented by the equation:

$Y=\beta 0+\beta 1X+\Box Y = \beta\_0 + \beta\_1 X + \epsilon Y=\beta 0+\beta 1 X+\Box$

Where:

- YYY is the dependent variable (e.g., sales revenue).
- XXX is the independent variable (e.g., advertising budget).
- $β0\beta\_0β0$ is the intercept of the line (the value of YYY when $X=0X = 0X=0$).
- $β1\beta\_1β1$ is the slope of the line (indicating the change in YYY for each unit change in XXX).
- $□\epsilon□$ is the error term (representing unexplained variance).

In multiple linear regression, there are multiple independent variables, and the model looks like this:

$Y=β0+β1X1+β2X2+\cdots+βnXn+□Y = \beta\_0 + \beta\_1 X\_1 + \beta\_2 X\_2 + \cdots + \beta\_n X\_n + \epsilon Y=β0+β1X1 +β2X2+\cdots+βnXn+□$

Where:

- $X1,X2,\cdots,XnX\_1, X\_2, \cdots, X\_nX1,X2,\cdots,Xn$ are the multiple input features.
- $β1,β2,\cdots,βn\beta\_1, \beta\_2, \cdots, \beta\_nβ1,β2 ,\cdots,βn$ are the corresponding coefficients for each feature.

The goal of linear regression is to find the best-fitting line (or hyperplane in multiple dimensions) that minimizes the difference between the predicted values and the actual observed values.

---

2. Building a Linear Regression Model

To build a linear regression model in Python using Scikit-learn, follow these steps:

2.1 Import Required Libraries

You will need Scikit-learn's `LinearRegression` class and other utilities such as `train_test_split` for splitting the data.

python

```
import pandas as pd
from sklearn.model_selection import train_test_split
from sklearn.linear_model import LinearRegression
from sklearn.metrics import mean_squared_error,
r2_score
```

2.2 Load and Prepare the Data

For this example, assume you have a dataset containing sales data and the corresponding advertising budget.

python

```
# Load the dataset (example data)
data = pd.read_csv('sales_data.csv')
```

```python
# Define independent variable (X) and dependent
variable (Y)
X = data[['Advertising_Budget']]   # Independent
variable (Advertising Budget)
Y = data['Sales_Revenue']          # Dependent
variable (Sales Revenue)
```

2.3 Split the Data

You can split the data into training and testing sets using Scikit-learn's `train_test_split`.

python

```python
X_train, X_test, Y_train, Y_test =
train_test_split(X, Y, test_size=0.2,
random_state=42)
```

2.4 Train the Model

Next, initialize the linear regression model and train it on the training data.

python

```python
# Initialize the Linear Regression model
model = LinearRegression()

# Train the model
model.fit(X_train, Y_train)
```

2.5 Make Predictions

Once the model is trained, you can use it to predict the sales revenue based on the advertising budget in the test set.

python

```
# Make predictions on the test set
Y_pred = model.predict(X_test)
```

3. Evaluating the Model Performance

To evaluate how well your linear regression model performs, you can use various metrics. Two common evaluation metrics are R^2 (R-squared) and **Mean Squared Error (MSE)**.

3.1 R^2 (R-squared)

R^2 is a statistical measure that explains how well the regression model fits the data. It is the proportion of the variance in the dependent variable that is predictable from the independent variables. R^2 ranges from 0 to 1:

- A value of **1** indicates a perfect fit (i.e., the model explains all the variance).
- A value of **0** indicates that the model explains none of the variance.

You can calculate R^2 using the `r2_score` function from Scikit-learn.

python

```
# Calculate R²
r2 = r2_score(Y_test, Y_pred)
print(f'R²: {r2:.2f}')
```

3.2 Mean Squared Error (MSE)

Mean Squared Error (MSE) is the average squared difference between the actual and predicted values. It provides an indication of how far off your predictions are from the true values. Lower MSE values indicate better performance. You can calculate MSE as follows:

```
python
```

```
# Calculate MSE
mse = mean_squared_error(Y_test, Y_pred)
print(f'Mean Squared Error (MSE): {mse:.2f}')
```

4. Real-World Example: Predicting Sales Revenue Based on Advertising Budget

Let's walk through a real-world example. Suppose you are working with a marketing team that wants to predict the **sales revenue** based on the **advertising budget**. The dataset contains information about how much was spent on advertising each month and the corresponding sales revenue.

4.1 Data Exploration

Before building the model, you would typically perform some exploratory data analysis (EDA) to understand the relationships between the variables. You may visualize the data using scatter plots to see if there is a linear relationship between advertising budget and sales revenue.

```python
import matplotlib.pyplot as plt
import seaborn as sns

# Visualize the relationship between Advertising
Budget and Sales Revenue
sns.scatterplot(x='Advertising_Budget',
y='Sales_Revenue', data=data)
plt.title('Advertising Budget vs Sales Revenue')
plt.xlabel('Advertising Budget ($)')
plt.ylabel('Sales Revenue ($)')
plt.show()
```

4.2 Model Building and Evaluation

After splitting the data and training the model, you will evaluate its performance using R^2 and MSE. Based on the performance, you may decide whether the model is good enough or whether additional features (like marketing channel, seasonality, etc.) are needed to improve predictions.

4.3 Prediction

Once the model is trained and evaluated, you can use it to predict future sales revenue based on new advertising budgets.

python

```
# Predict sales revenue for a new advertising budget
new_ad_budget = [[15000]]    # Example: $15,000
advertising budget
predicted_sales = model.predict(new_ad_budget)
print(f'Predicted          Sales          Revenue:
${predicted_sales[0]:,.2f}')
```

5.

Linear regression is a powerful and easy-to-implement algorithm for predicting continuous outcomes. By understanding how to build and evaluate linear regression models, you can apply them to a wide variety of real-world problems, from predicting house prices to forecasting sales revenue. While linear regression is simple, its application can provide valuable insights and form the foundation for more complex predictive models. In the next chapter, we will dive into other supervised learning algorithms, such as **decision trees** and **random forests**, which can handle more complex relationships and perform well in a variety of scenarios.

Chapter 11: Logistic Regression: Classification for Binary Outcomes

Logistic regression is a widely used algorithm for binary classification tasks in machine learning. Unlike linear regression, which is used for predicting continuous values, logistic regression is used to predict discrete outcomes, typically binary outcomes (e.g., yes/no, true/false, 0/1). In this chapter, we will cover the key steps in building and interpreting a logistic regression model, evaluating its performance using metrics like **accuracy**, **precision**, **recall**, and **F1-score**, and walk through a real-world example of classifying whether a **customer will purchase a product** based on various features.

---

1. What is Logistic Regression?

Logistic regression is a statistical method for analyzing datasets where the dependent variable is binary (i.e., it can take two possible outcomes). The model predicts the probability that an observation belongs to a particular class, typically represented by a value between 0 and 1.

The logistic function (also called the **sigmoid function**) is used to map any real-valued number into the range between 0 and 1. The function is defined as:

$P(Y=1|X)=11+e-(\beta 0+\beta 1X)P(Y = 1 | X) = \frac{1}{1 + e^{-(\beta_0 + \beta_1 X)}}P(Y=1|X)=1+e-(\beta 0+\beta 1X)1$

Where:

- $P(Y=1|X)P(Y = 1 | X)P(Y=1|X)$ is the probability that the output is 1 (e.g., the customer will purchase).
- $\beta 0\beta_0\beta 0$ is the intercept (bias term).
- $\beta 1\beta_1\beta 1$ is the coefficient (weight) associated with the feature XXX.
- XXX is the input feature (e.g., customer age, income, etc.).
- eee is Euler's number (the base of the natural logarithm).

The logistic function outputs a probability value between 0 and 1, which can be interpreted as the likelihood of the event happening (e.g., the likelihood of a customer purchasing a product).

To classify the outcome, a decision boundary is set, typically at 0.5. If the predicted probability is greater than or equal to 0.5, the model classifies the observation as 1 (purchase); if it is less than 0.5, it classifies the observation as 0 (no purchase).

---

2. Building a Logistic Regression Model

To build a logistic regression model in Python using Scikit-learn, follow these steps:

2.1 Import Required Libraries

You'll need Scikit-learn's `LogisticRegression` class and other utilities such as `train_test_split` for splitting the data.

python

```
import pandas as pd
from sklearn.model_selection import train_test_split
from sklearn.linear_model import LogisticRegression
from    sklearn.metrics    import    accuracy_score,
precision_score, recall_score, f1_score
```

2.2 Load and Prepare the Data

Assume you have a dataset with features that might influence whether a customer will purchase a product, such as age, income, and browsing history.

python

```
# Load the dataset (example data)
data = pd.read_csv('customer_data.csv')

# Define independent variables (X) and dependent
variable (y)
X = data[['Age', 'Income', 'Browsing_History']]   #
Independent variables
```

```
y = data['Purchased']   # Dependent variable (0 = no,
1 = yes)
```

2.3 Split the Data

As always, we split the data into training and testing sets to ensure that the model generalizes well.

python

```
X_train,      X_test,      y_train,      y_test      =
train_test_split(X,        y,            test_size=0.2,
random_state=42)
```

2.4 Train the Model

Initialize and fit the logistic regression model using the training data.

python

```
# Initialize the Logistic Regression model
model = LogisticRegression()

# Train the model
model.fit(X_train, y_train)
```

2.5 Make Predictions

Once the model is trained, we can use it to make predictions on the test data.

python

```
# Make predictions on the test set
y_pred = model.predict(X_test)
```

---

3. Evaluating Model Performance

Once we have trained the model and made predictions, it's essential to evaluate how well the model performs. The following metrics are commonly used to assess the performance of a logistic regression model:

3.1 Accuracy

Accuracy measures the proportion of correct predictions (both true positives and true negatives) among all predictions.

Accuracy=True Positives+True NegativesTotal Observations \text{Accuracy} = \frac{\text{True Positives} + \text{True Negatives}}{\text{Total Observations}}Accuracy=Total ObservationsTrue Positives+ True Negatives

While accuracy is a useful metric, it can be misleading when dealing with imbalanced datasets (e.g., if only a small percentage of customers purchase the product). In such cases, other metrics like precision and recall are more informative.

```python
accuracy = accuracy_score(y_test, y_pred)
print(f"Accuracy: {accuracy:.2f}")
```

3.2 Precision

Precision is the ratio of true positive predictions to the total number of positive predictions. It answers the question: **Of all the customers predicted to purchase the product, how many actually did?**

Precision=True PositivesTrue Positives+False Positives\text{ Precision} = \frac{\text{True Positives}}{\text{True Positives} + \text{False Positives}}Precision=True Positives+False PositivesTrue Positives

Precision is particularly important when the cost of false positives (e.g., predicting a customer will buy but they do not) is high.

python

```
precision = precision_score(y_test, y_pred)
print(f"Precision: {precision:.2f}")
```

3.3 Recall

Recall (or Sensitivity) is the ratio of true positive predictions to the total number of actual positive cases. It answers the question: **Of all the customers who actually purchased the product, how many did the model correctly predict?**

Recall=True PositivesTrue Positives+False Negatives\text{Recall} = \frac{\text{True Positives}}{\text{True Positives} + \text{False

Negatives}}Recall=True Positives+False NegativesTrue Positives

Recall is critical when the cost of false negatives (e.g., missing a potential customer) is high.

```python
recall = recall_score(y_test, y_pred)
print(f"Recall: {recall:.2f}")
```

3.4 F1-Score

The F1-score is the harmonic mean of precision and recall. It is a balanced measure that takes both false positives and false negatives into account.

F1-Score=2×Precision×RecallPrecision+RecallF1\text{-Score} = 2 \times \frac{\text{Precision} \times \text{Recall}}{\text{Precision} + \text{Recall}}F1-Score=2×Precision+RecallPrecision×Recall

The F1-score is particularly useful when you need a balance between precision and recall, especially in cases where the data is imbalanced.

```python
f1 = f1_score(y_test, y_pred)
print(f"F1-Score: {f1:.2f}")
```

4. Real-World Example: Classifying Whether a Customer Will Purchase a Product

In a real-world e-commerce setting, companies often want to predict whether a customer will purchase a product based on their demographic and behavioral data. For example, we can use features such as the customer's **age**, **income**, and **browsing history** to predict whether they will purchase a particular product.

By training a logistic regression model on this data, we can estimate the likelihood that a customer will make a purchase, and use that information to target customers more effectively with personalized marketing strategies. This could lead to increased sales and better resource allocation.

```python
# Example data
data = pd.DataFrame({
    'Age': [25, 34, 45, 23, 50],
    'Income': [50000, 60000, 80000, 35000, 120000],
    'Browsing_History': [5, 10, 3, 8, 15],
    'Purchased': [0, 1, 1, 0, 1]
})

# Features and target
X = data[['Age', 'Income', 'Browsing_History']]
y = data['Purchased']
```

```
# Train-test split, model building, and evaluation
can be done as discussed earlier
```

5.

Logistic regression is a powerful and interpretable model for binary classification tasks. By training a logistic regression model, you can predict whether an event will happen or not, such as whether a customer will purchase a product. Evaluating your model's performance using metrics like accuracy, precision, recall, and F1-score allows you to understand the model's strengths and weaknesses, especially in cases where the data may be imbalanced. With this foundational understanding, you can apply logistic regression to a wide range of binary classification problems in various domains such as marketing, finance, healthcare, and more.

Chapter 12: Decision Trees: Understanding Classification and Regression

Decision trees are a powerful and widely used machine learning algorithm, both for classification and regression tasks. These models are easy to understand, interpret, and visualize. They work by recursively splitting the data into subsets based on the most significant features, using criteria such as **information gain** or **Gini impurity** (for classification) or **mean squared error** (for regression). In this chapter, we will cover the core concepts of decision trees, how they are used for both classification and regression, and how to prevent overfitting by tuning hyperparameters. We will walk through a real-world example of predicting **employee performance** using decision trees.

---

1. What is a Decision Tree?

A **decision tree** is a tree-like structure where each internal node represents a **decision** based on a feature (e.g., age, income), each branch represents the outcome of the decision, and each leaf node represents a **prediction** or **output**.

- **For classification** tasks, the leaf nodes represent the class labels.

- **For regression** tasks, the leaf nodes represent continuous values (predicted output).

The goal of a decision tree algorithm is to recursively split the dataset into subsets that are as homogeneous as possible with respect to the target variable.

---

2. Decision Trees for Classification

In classification, a decision tree works by splitting the data at each node based on the feature that best separates the different classes. Common splitting criteria include:

- **Gini Impurity**: Measures how often a randomly chosen element would be incorrectly classified if it was randomly labeled according to the distribution of labels in the dataset. It is used in algorithms like the **CART (Classification and Regression Trees)** method.
- **Entropy and Information Gain**: Measures the amount of "disorder" or uncertainty in the data. Information gain is the reduction in entropy when splitting on a feature.

For example, if we wanted to predict whether a customer will buy a product (binary classification: "yes" or "no"), the decision tree might first split on the "age" feature, then on "income," and so on, until it arrives at a decision.

Example:

A decision tree might look like this for predicting whether a customer will buy a product:

- If **Age > 30**:
    - If **Income > 50,000** → "Buy"
    - If **Income ≤ 50,000** → "Don't Buy"
- If **Age ≤ 30** → "Don't Buy"

---

3. Decision Trees for Regression

In regression, decision trees predict a continuous output rather than discrete classes. The goal is to split the dataset in a way that minimizes the variance of the target variable within each subset. A regression tree will predict the average of the target values in each leaf node.

Example:

If we wanted to predict a continuous variable like **employee performance**, the tree might split based on features such as age, years of experience, or education level. Each leaf node would contain the average performance score for employees in that subset.

---

4. Building a Decision Tree Model

4.1 Import Required Libraries

To build decision trees, we need the `DecisionTreeClassifier` (for classification) or `DecisionTreeRegressor` (for regression) from Scikit-learn.

python

```
from sklearn.tree import DecisionTreeClassifier,
DecisionTreeRegressor
from sklearn.model_selection import train_test_split
from sklearn.metrics import accuracy_score,
mean_squared_error
import pandas as pd
```

4.2 Load and Prepare the Data

Let's assume we have a dataset that contains features of employees, such as age, years of experience, and education level, along with their performance scores. The task is to predict employee performance using decision trees.

python

```
# Load the dataset (example data)
data = pd.read_csv('employee_performance.csv')

# Define features (X) and target (y)
X = data[['Age', 'Experience', 'Education_Level']]  #
Features
```

```
y = data['Performance_Score']   # Target variable
(performance score)
```

4.3 Split the Data

We will split the data into training and testing sets.

python

```
X_train,    X_test,    y_train,    y_test    =
train_test_split(X,        y,         test_size=0.2,
random_state=42)
```

4.4 Train the Model

For **classification**, use `DecisionTreeClassifier`, and for **regression**, use `DecisionTreeRegressor`.

python

```
# For classification:
model = DecisionTreeClassifier(random_state=42)
model.fit(X_train, y_train)

# For regression:
# model = DecisionTreeRegressor(random_state=42)
# model.fit(X_train, y_train)
```

4.5 Make Predictions

After training the model, we can make predictions on the test set.

python

```
y_pred = model.predict(X_test)
```

5. Evaluating the Model Performance

5.1 Classification Model Evaluation

For classification tasks, we typically evaluate the model using metrics like **accuracy**, **precision**, **recall**, and **F1-score**.

python

```python
accuracy = accuracy_score(y_test, y_pred)
print(f'Accuracy: {accuracy:.2f}')
```

5.2 Regression Model Evaluation

For regression tasks, we use metrics like **Mean Squared Error (MSE)** and R^2 to evaluate model performance.

python

```python
# For regression tasks
mse = mean_squared_error(y_test, y_pred)
r2 = model.score(X_test, y_test)    # R² score
print(f'Mean Squared Error: {mse:.2f}')
print(f'R²: {r2:.2f}')
```

6. Tuning Decision Tree Hyperparameters

One common issue with decision trees is **overfitting**, especially when the tree is allowed to grow too deep. Overfitting occurs when the model learns the noise in the training data rather than the underlying patterns. This can be addressed by tuning the tree's hyperparameters to limit its complexity. Some common hyperparameters to tune include:

- **max_depth**: The maximum depth of the tree.
- **min_samples_split**: The minimum number of samples required to split an internal node.
- **min_samples_leaf**: The minimum number of samples required to be at a leaf node.
- **max_features**: The number of features to consider when looking for the best split.

Here's how you can tune these hyperparameters:

```python
python

# Initialize the DecisionTreeClassifier with hyperparameters
model = DecisionTreeClassifier(max_depth=5, min_samples_split=10, min_samples_leaf=5, random_state=42)

# Train the model with the training data
model.fit(X_train, y_train)
```

You can also use **cross-validation** to find the optimal hyperparameters using tools like `GridSearchCV` or `RandomizedSearchCV` in Scikit-learn.

7. Real-World Example: Predicting Employee Performance Using Decision Trees

In this real-world example, we aim to predict **employee performance** based on features such as age, years of experience, and education level.

- **Problem**: A company wants to identify employees who are likely to have low performance scores so that they can take corrective actions (training, reassignment, etc.).

- **Solution**: We will use a decision tree model to classify employees based on their features and predict whether their performance score is high or low.

Steps:

1. **Data Preparation**: Import and clean employee data, including features like age, years of experience, and education level.

2. **Model Building**: Train a decision tree classifier on this data.

3. **Evaluation**: Evaluate the model's accuracy, precision, recall, and F1-score.

4. **Hyperparameter Tuning**: Use hyperparameter tuning to prevent overfitting and improve model performance.

8.

Decision trees are a powerful tool for both classification and regression tasks. By splitting the data into subsets based on the most informative features, decision trees can provide clear insights into the relationships between input features and the target variable. With proper tuning, decision trees can handle complex datasets and make accurate predictions.

Chapter 13: Support Vector Machines (SVM)

Support Vector Machines (SVMs) are powerful supervised learning algorithms used primarily for classification tasks, though they can also be applied to regression problems. SVMs are known for their ability to handle high-dimensional data and create complex decision boundaries, making them a popular choice for problems like text classification, image recognition, and bioinformatics. In this chapter, we will introduce the key concepts behind SVMs—hyperplanes, kernels, and margins—demonstrate how to build an SVM classifier using Scikit-learn, and walk through a real-world example of classifying **email spam vs. non-spam**.

---

1. What is a Support Vector Machine?

An SVM is a supervised learning algorithm used to classify data by finding a hyperplane that best separates different classes in the feature space. The key idea behind SVMs is to maximize the **margin** between the classes, which improves the generalization ability of the model.

- **Hyperplane**: In a 2D space, a hyperplane is a line that divides the space into two regions, each representing one class. In higher dimensions, a hyperplane is a plane (in 3D) or a hyperplane in higher dimensions (in n-D).

- **Margin**: The margin is the distance between the closest data points from each class to the hyperplane. The greater the margin, the better the model is at generalizing, which means fewer errors on unseen data.

- **Support Vectors**: The support vectors are the data points that lie closest to the hyperplane and influence its position and orientation. These are the critical elements that define the optimal hyperplane.

SVMs aim to find the hyperplane that maximizes the margin, which can be formalized as an optimization problem. When data is not linearly separable, SVM uses a technique called the **kernel trick** to map data into higher-dimensional spaces where it becomes easier to separate the classes.

---

2. Types of SVMs

- **Linear SVM**: When the data is linearly separable, SVM finds a linear hyperplane to separate the classes.

- **Non-linear SVM**: When the data is not linearly separable, SVM uses **kernels** to transform the data into a higher-dimensional space where a linear separation becomes possible. The most commonly used kernels are:

- o **Polynomial Kernel**: $K(x,x')=(x\cdot x'+1)dK(x, x') = (x \cdot x' + 1)^\wedge dK(x,x')=(x\cdot x'+1)d$, where ddd is the degree of the polynomial.

- o **Radial Basis Function (RBF) Kernel**: $K(x,x')=\exp[\![\overline{\omega}]\!](-\gamma\|x-x'\|2)K(x, x') = \exp\left(-\gamma \| x - x' \|^\wedge 2\right)K(x,x')=\exp(-\gamma\|x-x'\|2)$, where γ\gammaγ is a hyperparameter that controls the width of the Gaussian function.

---

3. Building an SVM Classifier with Scikit-learn

3.1 Importing Required Libraries

To build an SVM model in Python, we need to import necessary libraries from Scikit-learn. We will use svc for classification (Support Vector Classification).

python

```
from sklearn.svm import SVC
from sklearn.model_selection import train_test_split
from sklearn.metrics import accuracy_score,
classification_report
from sklearn.feature_extraction.text import
TfidfVectorizer
import pandas as pd
```

3.2 Loading and Preparing the Data

Let's assume we are working with a dataset that contains email data labeled as **spam** or **non-spam**. The goal is to classify emails based on features like the presence of specific words or phrases.

python

```
# Load the dataset (example data)
data = pd.read_csv('email_data.csv')   # Columns:
'text' (email content), 'label' (spam or not)

# Convert the 'label' to binary values: 1 for spam, 0
for non-spam
data['label'] = data['label'].map({'spam': 1, 'non-
spam': 0})

# Define features (X) and target (y)
X = data['text']  # Email content
y = data['label']  # Target variable (spam = 1, non-
spam = 0)
```

3.3 Text Feature Extraction

Since we are working with text data, we need to convert the email text into numerical features. We will use **TF-IDF (Term Frequency-Inverse Document Frequency)** to represent the words in the emails.

python

```
# Convert text data into numerical features using TF-
IDF Vectorizer
vectorizer  =  TfidfVectorizer(stop_words='english',
max_features=5000)  # Limit to 5000 features
X = vectorizer.fit_transform(X)
```

3.4 Splitting the Data

We will split the data into training and testing sets to evaluate the performance of the model.

python

```
# Split the data into training and testing sets
X_train,    X_test,    y_train,    y_test    =
train_test_split(X,    y,    test_size=0.2,
random_state=42)
```

3.5 Training the Model

Now, we can initialize and train the **SVC** model with a **Radial Basis Function (RBF)** kernel, which is commonly used for non-linear classification.

python

```
# Initialize the SVM model with RBF kernel
model = SVC(kernel='rbf', C=1, gamma=0.1)  # C is the
regularization parameter, gamma controls the kernel
width

# Train the model
model.fit(X_train, y_train)
```

3.6 Making Predictions

Once the model is trained, we can use it to predict whether new emails are spam or not.

python

```
# Make predictions on the test set
y_pred = model.predict(X_test)
```

---

4. Evaluating the Model Performance

To evaluate how well our SVM model performs, we will use several classification metrics, including **accuracy**, **precision**, **recall**, and **F1-score**. These metrics help us understand the trade-offs between correctly identifying spam (precision) and minimizing false negatives (recall).

4.1 Accuracy

Accuracy is the proportion of correct predictions out of all predictions.

python

```
accuracy = accuracy_score(y_test, y_pred)
print(f"Accuracy: {accuracy * 100:.2f}%")
```

4.2 Precision, Recall, and F1-Score

- **Precision**: The proportion of correctly predicted spam emails out of all emails predicted as spam.

- **Recall**: The proportion of correctly predicted spam emails out of all actual spam emails.
- **F1-Score**: The harmonic mean of precision and recall, balancing both metrics.

python

```
print("Classification Report:")
print(classification_report(y_test, y_pred))
```

5. Real-World Example: Classifying Email Spam vs. Non-Spam

In this real-world example, we applied an SVM classifier to classify emails as **spam** or **non-spam** based on their content. The process involved:

- **Loading the dataset** containing email text and labels (spam/non-spam).
- **Preprocessing the text** data by converting it into numerical features using **TF-IDF**.
- **Splitting the data** into training and testing sets.
- **Training an SVM classifier** with an RBF kernel.
- **Evaluating model performance** using classification metrics such as accuracy, precision, recall, and F1-score.

In practice, SVMs can be fine-tuned by experimenting with different kernels, regularization parameters (CCC), and kernel parameters (γ\gamma$\gamma$) to achieve better performance on more complex datasets.

6.

Support Vector Machines are powerful models for both linear and non-linear classification tasks. They excel in high-dimensional spaces, making them ideal for text classification problems like spam detection. By understanding the key concepts behind SVMs—hyperplanes, margins, and kernels—you can effectively apply them to a wide range of real-world machine learning tasks. In this chapter, we demonstrated how to implement an SVM classifier using Scikit-learn and evaluated its performance for the email spam classification problem.

Chapter 14: k-Nearest Neighbors (k-NN)

The **k-Nearest Neighbors (k-NN)** algorithm is one of the simplest and most intuitive machine learning algorithms. It belongs to the **instance-based learning** family, meaning it makes predictions based on the similarity (distance) between the data points in the feature space. k-NN can be used for both **classification** and **regression** tasks, but it is more commonly used for classification. In this chapter, we will explain how k-NN works, how to evaluate its performance, and how to select the optimal value of kkk. We will walk through a real-world example of classifying different **types of flowers** using the **Iris dataset**.

---

1. What is k-Nearest Neighbors (k-NN)?

The k-NN algorithm classifies a new data point based on the majority class of its **k** closest data points. The algorithm works under the assumption that similar instances (data points) are likely to have the same class label. The **k** parameter represents the number of neighbors to consider when making a prediction.

- **Classification**: If kkk nearest neighbors belong to different classes, the class that appears the most (the majority class) is assigned to the new data point.

- **Regression**: For regression tasks, the predicted value is the average (or weighted average) of the values of the k nearest neighbors.

The proximity between data points is typically measured using a **distance metric**, with **Euclidean distance** being the most common.

Euclidean Distance between two points $p1=(x1,y1)p\_1 = (x\_1, y\_1)p1=(x1,y1)$ and $p2=(x2,y2)p\_2 = (x\_2, y\_2)p2=(x2,y2)$ in a 2D space is given by:

$$d(p1,p2)=(x2-x1)2+(y2-y1)2d(p\_1, p\_2) = \sqrt{(x\_2 - x\_1)^2 + (y\_2 - y\_1)^2}d(p1,p2)=(x2-x1)2+(y2-y1)2$$

k-NN is a **lazy learner** because it doesn't learn an explicit model from the training data. Instead, it stores the training data and makes predictions based on the proximity of new data points.

---

2. Building and Understanding the k-NN Algorithm

2.1 How k-NN Works:

1. **Training Phase**: There is no explicit training phase for k-NN. It simply stores the training data in memory.
2. **Prediction Phase**: When a new data point needs to be classified, the algorithm:

- Computes the distance between the new point and all points in the training set.
- Sorts the distances and selects the **k** nearest neighbors.
- Assigns the majority class (for classification) or average value (for regression) of the **k** neighbors to the new data point.

2.2 Choosing the Right Distance Metric:

The default distance metric is **Euclidean distance**, but other metrics such as **Manhattan distance** (sum of absolute differences) or **Minkowski distance** (a generalized form of Euclidean and Manhattan) can be used depending on the problem.

- **Euclidean   Distance:**
  $d(p1,p2)=(x2-x1)2+(y2-y1)2d(p\_1, p\_2) = \sqrt{(x\_2 - x\_1)^2 + (y\_2 - y\_1)^2}d(p1,p2)=(x2-x1)2+(y2-y1)2$
- **Manhattan   Distance:**
  $d(p1,p2)=|x2-x1|+|y2-y1|d(p\_1, p\_2) = |x\_2 - x\_1| + |y\_2 - y\_1|d(p1,p2)=|x2-x1|+|y2-y1|$

2.3 Choosing the Right k Value:

- **Small k values (e.g., 1):** The model may be too sensitive to noise and can overfit.
- **Large k values:** The model may become too simple, leading to underfitting.

- **Optimal k**: The best k is often determined by using techniques like **cross-validation**.

---

3. Evaluating Model Performance and Choosing the Optimal k Value

3.1 Model Performance Evaluation:

The performance of a k-NN classifier can be evaluated using metrics such as **accuracy**, **precision**, **recall**, and **F1-score**. Additionally, it is important to check the **confusion matrix** to understand how well the model is classifying the data.

3.2 Cross-Validation for Optimal k:

To determine the optimal value of kkk, it's common to use **cross-validation** to assess model performance for different values of kkk. The optimal kkk minimizes overfitting and underfitting.

---

4. Building a k-NN Model with Scikit-learn

4.1 Importing Required Libraries

To build a k-NN classifier in Python, we need Scikit-learn's `KNeighborsClassifier`:

```python
```

```
from sklearn.neighbors import KNeighborsClassifier
```

```
from sklearn.model_selection import train_test_split,
cross_val_score
from sklearn.metrics import accuracy_score
import pandas as pd
```

4.2 Load and Prepare the Data

Let's use the **Iris dataset**, which contains 150 samples of iris flowers, each with 4 features: sepal length, sepal width, petal length, and petal width. The task is to classify the flowers into one of three species: **Setosa**, **Versicolor**, or **Virginica**.

python

```
# Load the Iris dataset
from sklearn.datasets import load_iris
data = load_iris()
X = data.data   # Features (sepal length, width, petal
length, width)
y = data.target   # Target variable (species)

# Split data into training and testing sets
X_train,     X_test,     y_train,     y_test     =
train_test_split(X,        y,           test_size=0.3,
random_state=42)
```

4.3 Build and Train the k-NN Model

We will build the model using k-NN with a chosen value of k (e.g., k=3k = 3k=3).

python

```
# Initialize the k-NN model with k=3
knn = KNeighborsClassifier(n_neighbors=3)

# Train the model
knn.fit(X_train, y_train)
```

4.4 Make Predictions and Evaluate the Model

Once the model is trained, we can evaluate its performance on the test set using accuracy and cross-validation.

python

```
# Make predictions
y_pred = knn.predict(X_test)

# Evaluate the model's performance
accuracy = accuracy_score(y_test, y_pred)
print(f'Accuracy: {accuracy:.2f}')
```

4.5 Finding the Optimal k using Cross-Validation

We can evaluate different values of kkk and select the one that gives the best performance.

python

```
# Try different k values using cross-validation
k_values = range(1, 21)
cv_scores                                        =
[cross_val_score(KNeighborsClassifier(n_neighbors=k),
X, y, cv=5).mean() for k in k_values]
```

```
# Plot the results to find the best k
import matplotlib.pyplot as plt
plt.plot(k_values, cv_scores)
plt.xlabel('k')
plt.ylabel('Cross-Validation Accuracy')
plt.title('Optimal k for k-NN')
plt.show()
```

5. Real-World Example: Classifying Types of Flowers Using the Iris Dataset

The **Iris dataset** is a classic example in machine learning for demonstrating classification techniques. The dataset contains three species of Iris flowers—Setosa, Versicolor, and Virginica—with four features: sepal length, sepal width, petal length, and petal width. Our task is to classify the flowers into one of these species based on the features.

In the example above, we:

- Loaded and preprocessed the data.
- Built a k-NN classifier.
- Evaluated the model performance.
- Used cross-validation to select the optimal kkk.

This demonstrates how k-NN can be effectively used for classification tasks, especially when the data has multiple features and the decision boundary is not easily separable by a linear classifier.

6.

The k-Nearest Neighbors algorithm is a simple yet powerful method for both classification and regression tasks. Its performance heavily depends on choosing the right distance metric and the optimal kkk value. In this chapter, we introduced the theory behind k-NN, built a classifier using Scikit-learn, and applied it to the Iris dataset for classifying types of flowers. By experimenting with different kkk values, we can optimize the model to balance between underfitting and overfitting.

In the next chapter, we will explore **Ensemble Learning** techniques, which combine multiple models to improve performance and reduce the risk of overfitting.

Chapter 15: Model Evaluation: Assessing Performance

Model evaluation is a critical step in the machine learning pipeline. After training a model, we need to assess its performance to ensure it makes accurate predictions. This chapter covers different metrics for evaluating both **regression** and **classification** models, introduces **cross-validation** as a powerful tool for model validation, and walks through a real-world example of evaluating a machine learning model for **customer satisfaction prediction**.

---

1. Why Model Evaluation is Important

Model evaluation helps in understanding how well a machine learning model generalizes to unseen data. While training a model is crucial, assessing its ability to make predictions on new data ensures it is not overfitting (memorizing the training data) or underfitting (failing to capture patterns). The goal is to find a model that balances **bias** and **variance**, leading to better generalization.

- **Bias**: Error due to overly simplistic assumptions made by the model.
- **Variance**: Error due to the model being too complex and overfitting to the noise in the data.

2. Metrics for Evaluating Regression Models

For **regression** models, where the goal is to predict a continuous variable (e.g., predicting sales revenue or house prices), several evaluation metrics can help assess the model's performance:

2.1 Mean Absolute Error (MAE)

MAE is the average of the absolute differences between predicted and actual values. It gives us an idea of the magnitude of the errors in predictions.

$$\text{MAE} = \frac{1}{n} \sum_{i=1}^{n} |y_i - \hat{y}_i|$$

Where:

- y_i is the actual value.
- $\hat{y}_i$ is the predicted value.
- n is the number of data points.

2.2 Mean Squared Error (MSE)

MSE penalizes larger errors more heavily by squaring the differences between predicted and actual values. It is more sensitive to outliers compared to MAE.

$$\text{MSE} = \frac{1}{n} \sum_{i=1}^{n} (y_i - \hat{y}_i)^2$$

2.3 R-squared (R^2)

R^2 measures the proportion of variance in the dependent variable that is predictable from the independent variables. An R^2 value closer to 1 indicates that the model explains most of the variance, while a value closer to 0 indicates poor model fit.

$$R2=1-\sum i=1 n(yi-y^i)2\sum i=1 n(yi-y^-)2 R^2 \quad = \quad 1 -$$
$$\frac{\sum_{i=1}^{n} (y_i - \hat{y}_i)^2}{\sum_{i=1}^{n} (y_i - \bar{y})^2} R2=1-\sum i=1 n(yi-y^-)2\sum i=1 n(yi-y^i)2$$

Where:

- yiy_iyi is the actual value.
- $y^i\hat{y}_iy^i$ is the predicted value.
- $y^-\bar{y}y^-$ is the mean of actual values.

---

3. Metrics for Evaluating Classification Models

For **classification** models, where the goal is to classify data points into discrete categories (e.g., spam vs. non-spam, customer churn prediction), we use the following evaluation metrics:

3.1 Accuracy

Accuracy is the most straightforward metric, representing the proportion of correct predictions to total predictions:

Accuracy=Number of Correct PredictionsTotal Number of Pr edictions\text{Accuracy} = \frac{\text{Number of Correct Predictions}}{\text{Total Number of Predictions}}Accuracy=Total Number of PredictionsNumber of Correct Predictions

However, accuracy can be misleading, especially with imbalanced datasets (e.g., predicting whether a customer will churn, where most customers do not churn).

3.2 Precision, Recall, and F1-Score

- **Precision**: Measures how many of the predicted positive cases were actually positive. It is useful when the cost of false positives is high.

  Precision=True PositivesTrue Positives+False Positiv es\text{Precision} = \frac{\text{True Positives}}{\text{True Positives} + \text{False Positives}}Precision=True Positives+False PositivesTr ue Positives

- **Recall**: Measures how many of the actual positive cases were correctly identified by the model. It is useful when the cost of false negatives is high.

  Recall=True PositivesTrue Positives+False Negatives \text{Recall} = \frac{\text{True Positives}}{\text{True

Positives}   +   \text{False Negatives}}Recall=True Positives+False NegativesTrue Positives

- **F1-Score**: The harmonic mean of precision and recall, providing a balance between the two. It is particularly useful when dealing with imbalanced datasets.

F1-Score=2×Precision×RecallPrecision+Recall\text{F1-Score} = 2 \times \frac{\text{Precision} \times \text{Recall}}{\text{Precision} + \text{Recall}}F1-Score=2×Precision+RecallPrecision×Recall

3.3 ROC Curve and AUC

The **ROC (Receiver Operating Characteristic) curve** is a graphical representation of a classifier's performance across different thresholds. The **AUC (Area Under the Curve)** is the area under the ROC curve and provides an aggregate measure of the model's ability to distinguish between positive and negative classes.

---

4. Cross-Validation: Why It's Important for Model Evaluation

Cross-validation is a technique used to assess the generalization performance of a model by splitting the data into multiple subsets or folds. Instead of using a single train-test split, cross-validation trains the model multiple times on different subsets of the data, allowing for a more reliable estimate of performance.

4.1 K-Fold Cross-Validation

In **k-fold cross-validation**, the dataset is divided into **k** equally sized folds. The model is trained on **k-1** folds and tested on the remaining fold. This process is repeated **k** times, and the results are averaged to get a final performance estimate.

For example, in **5-fold cross-validation**:

- The data is split into 5 folds.
- The model is trained on 4 folds and tested on the 5th fold, rotating the test fold each time.

This method ensures that the model is tested on all data points and helps prevent overfitting.

4.2 Stratified Cross-Validation

In **stratified k-fold cross-validation**, the splits are made such that each fold contains the same proportion of class labels, which is especially useful in cases of imbalanced classes.

---

5. Real-World Example: Evaluating a Machine Learning Model for Customer Satisfaction Prediction

Let's say we're building a machine learning model to predict customer satisfaction based on features like purchase frequency, customer service interactions, and product reviews. Our model's performance can be evaluated using the following steps:

5.1 Loading the Data and Preparing Features

python

```
import pandas as pd
from sklearn.model_selection import train_test_split
from sklearn.ensemble import RandomForestClassifier
from sklearn.metrics import accuracy_score,
precision_score, recall_score, f1_score

# Load dataset (example data)
data = pd.read_csv('customer_satisfaction.csv')

# Features and target
X              =              data[['purchase_frequency',
'service_interaction', 'product_reviews']]
y = data['satisfaction_label']  # 1 for satisfied, 0
for unsatisfied

# Split data into training and testing sets
X_train,    X_test,    y_train,    y_test    =
train_test_split(X,        y,        test_size=0.2,
random_state=42)
```

5.2 Building the Model

python

```python
# Train a random forest classifier
model = RandomForestClassifier(random_state=42)
model.fit(X_train, y_train)

# Make predictions
y_pred = model.predict(X_test)
```

5.3 Evaluating the Model Performance

python

```python
# Evaluate using accuracy, precision, recall, and F1-
score
accuracy = accuracy_score(y_test, y_pred)
precision = precision_score(y_test, y_pred)
recall = recall_score(y_test, y_pred)
f1 = f1_score(y_test, y_pred)

print(f"Accuracy: {accuracy:.2f}")
print(f"Precision: {precision:.2f}")
print(f"Recall: {recall:.2f}")
print(f"F1-Score: {f1:.2f}")
```

5.4 Cross-Validation

To improve the reliability of the performance metrics, we use **cross-validation**:

python

```python
from sklearn.model_selection import cross_val_score
```

```python
# Perform 5-fold cross-validation
cv_scores = cross_val_score(model, X, y, cv=5)
print(f"Cross-validation scores: {cv_scores}")
print(f"Average CV score: {cv_scores.mean():.2f}")
```

6.

Effective model evaluation is essential to ensure that your machine learning models perform well and generalize to new, unseen data. By using appropriate metrics such as **accuracy**, **precision**, **recall**, **F1-score**, and **cross-validation**, you can better assess how well your model is likely to perform in the real world. Additionally, understanding the strengths and weaknesses of different evaluation metrics allows you to make informed decisions when tuning and selecting your models.

Chapter 16: Overfitting and Underfitting: Diagnosing and Improving Models

In machine learning, one of the most critical challenges is finding the right balance between **overfitting** and **underfitting**. Both problems can negatively impact the model's performance, and understanding them is essential to building effective and generalizable models. This chapter explains the concepts of overfitting and underfitting, introduces the **bias-variance trade-off**, and discusses techniques like **regularization** and **pruning** to improve model performance. We will also walk through a real-world example of **reducing overfitting** in a **decision tree** used for **loan approval** predictions.

---

1. The Bias-Variance Trade-Off

The **bias-variance trade-off** is a fundamental concept in machine learning that helps explain overfitting and underfitting.

- **Bias**: Bias refers to the error introduced by approximating a real-world problem (which may be complex) by a simplified model. High bias means the model makes strong assumptions and oversimplifies the data, which can lead to **underfitting**.

- o **Example**: A linear model trying to predict complex patterns in the data that are non-linear would exhibit high bias.
- **Variance**: Variance refers to the error introduced by the model's sensitivity to small fluctuations or noise in the training data. High variance means the model is overly complex and learns too much from the training data, including the noise, which can lead to **overfitting**.
  - o **Example**: A decision tree that grows too deep and fits perfectly to every training example, including outliers, would exhibit high variance.

The trade-off occurs because as you decrease bias (by making the model more complex), you typically increase variance, and vice versa. The goal is to find the optimal point where both bias and variance are balanced, resulting in a model that generalizes well to unseen data.

---

2. Overfitting and Underfitting: Understanding the Concepts

2.1 Overfitting

Overfitting happens when a model is too complex and captures noise or random fluctuations in the training data, rather than just the underlying patterns. This leads to great performance on the training set but poor performance on new, unseen data (i.e., the model doesn't generalize well).

- **Signs of Overfitting**:
  - High accuracy on the training data but low accuracy on validation or test data.
  - A model that's too complex, like a decision tree with many levels.
  - Overly sensitive predictions that change dramatically with small changes in the input data.

2.2 Underfitting

Underfitting occurs when a model is too simple to capture the underlying patterns in the data. It fails to learn the structure of the data, leading to poor performance on both the training and test datasets.

- **Signs of Underfitting**:
  - Low accuracy on both the training and test data.
  - A model that is too simple, such as a linear regression model trying to capture a non-linear relationship.

3. Techniques to Reduce Overfitting

To reduce overfitting, we need to make our model more generalizable by reducing its complexity. Several techniques can help:

3.1 Regularization

Regularization is a technique used to add a penalty to the model's complexity to prevent overfitting. Regularization methods discourage the model from fitting noise or irrelevant details in the training data.

- **L1 Regularization (Lasso)**: Lasso (Least Absolute Shrinkage and Selection Operator) adds a penalty equal to the absolute value of the coefficients to the cost function. It has the effect of driving some coefficients to zero, effectively performing feature selection.

  Cost Function with L1=Loss Function+$\lambda\sum$i=1n|wi|\text{ Cost Function with L1} = \text{Loss Function} + \lambda \sum_{i=1}^n |w_i|Cost Function with L1=Loss Function+λi=1$\sum$n|wi|

- **L2 Regularization (Ridge)**: Ridge regularization adds a penalty equal to the square of the coefficients. It helps prevent the coefficients from becoming too large and thus helps the model generalize better.

Cost Function with L2=Loss Function+λ∑i=1nwi2\text{ Cost Function with L2} = \text{Loss Function} + \lambda \sum_{i=1}^n w_i^2Cost Function with L2=Loss Function+λi=1∑n wi2

- **Elastic Net**: Combines L1 and L2 regularization, providing a balance between feature selection and coefficient shrinkage.

3.2 Pruning (for Decision Trees)

Pruning is a technique used to reduce the size of a decision tree after it's built. It involves removing parts of the tree that do not provide significant predictive power.

- **Pre-Pruning**: This technique stops the tree from growing beyond a certain depth or size during the construction phase.
- **Post-Pruning**: After the tree has been fully grown, pruning removes branches that have little contribution to the model's accuracy (e.g., branches that lead to overfitting the training data).

In decision trees, pruning is essential for improving generalization and reducing variance, as deeper trees with many nodes tend to overfit.

4. Real-World Example: Reducing Overfitting in a Decision Tree for Loan Approval

Let's consider a scenario where we are building a decision tree to predict whether a customer will be approved for a loan based on several features, such as income, age, credit score, and loan amount. A basic decision tree might overfit the training data if it grows too deep, capturing noise in the data rather than meaningful patterns.

4.1 Building the Initial Model

We begin by training a decision tree using the entire dataset. Initially, the tree fits the data well and achieves high accuracy on the training set. However, when we test the model on validation data, we observe a significant drop in accuracy, indicating overfitting.

python

```
from sklearn.tree import DecisionTreeClassifier
from sklearn.model_selection import train_test_split
from sklearn.metrics import accuracy_score

# Load the dataset
data = pd.read_csv('loan_data.csv')

# Features and target
X = data.drop('loan_approved', axis=1)
```

```
y = data['loan_approved']

# Split into training and testing sets
X_train,      X_test,      y_train,      y_test      =
train_test_split(X,           y,            test_size=0.3,
random_state=42)

# Initialize and fit the model
model = DecisionTreeClassifier(random_state=42)
model.fit(X_train, y_train)

# Predict on the test set
y_pred = model.predict(X_test)

# Evaluate accuracy
print("Accuracy:", accuracy_score(y_test, y_pred))
```

4.2 Pruning the Tree

To reduce overfitting, we apply pruning by limiting the tree's maximum depth and setting a minimum number of samples required to split a node.

python

```
# Apply pruning by setting parameters
model_pruned    =    DecisionTreeClassifier(max_depth=5,
min_samples_split=10, random_state=42)
model_pruned.fit(X_train, y_train)

# Predict on the test set with the pruned tree
y_pred_pruned = model_pruned.predict(X_test)
```

```
# Evaluate accuracy
print("Accuracy                    after                    pruning:",
accuracy_score(y_test, y_pred_pruned))
```

4.3 Comparing Results

After pruning, we expect the model's performance on the test set to improve, as it now generalizes better by not overfitting the training data. Pruning helps avoid overly complex trees that learn patterns specific to the training data.

5.

Overfitting and underfitting are two of the biggest challenges in machine learning. By understanding the **bias-variance trade-off** and applying techniques like **regularization** and **pruning**, we can build models that generalize well to new data. In practice, techniques such as **cross-validation**, **early stopping**, and **ensemble methods** can also be used to further improve the performance of our models. The key to building effective machine learning models is constant testing, tuning, and understanding the model's behavior on unseen data.

Chapter 17: Hyperparameter Tuning: Improving Model Accuracy

Hyperparameters are the parameters that are not learned during model training but are set before training begins. These parameters can have a significant impact on the model's performance, and selecting the right values for them is crucial to improving model accuracy. This chapter will cover **hyperparameter tuning** using methods like **Grid Search** and **Random Search**, and introduce tools like **GridSearchCV** and **RandomizedSearchCV** in Scikit-learn. We will also discuss how to tune hyperparameters for an **SVM model** to improve the prediction of customer churn.

---

1. What Are Hyperparameters?

In machine learning, **hyperparameters** are the configuration settings for the model that influence the learning process and model performance. Unlike **parameters** (such as weights in a neural network) which are learned from the data during training, hyperparameters are set prior to training.

Examples of hyperparameters include:

- **For linear models (e.g., Logistic Regression):** Regularization strength (λ\lambda$\lambda$) and solver type.

- **For decision trees**: Maximum depth of the tree, minimum samples per leaf.
- **For support vector machines (SVM)**: The regularization parameter CCC, the kernel type, and the kernel's specific parameters (e.g., gamma for the RBF kernel).

Finding the optimal values for these hyperparameters can significantly improve the model's accuracy and performance.

---

2. Methods for Hyperparameter Tuning

2.1 Grid Search

Grid search is an exhaustive search method that tests all possible combinations of a predefined set of hyperparameter values. While it can be computationally expensive, it ensures that the best combination of hyperparameters is found.

Steps involved in grid search:

1. Define a grid of possible hyperparameter values.
2. Train the model for every combination of values.
3. Evaluate the model using cross-validation (or a separate validation set) for each combination.
4. Select the hyperparameters that result in the best performance.

For example, if we are tuning an SVM, we might define a grid for CCC (regularization parameter) and **kernel type** as follows:

- C={0.01,0.1,1,10,100}C = \{0.01, 0.1, 1, 10, 100\}C={0.01,0.1,1,10,100}
- Kernel = {'linear', 'rbf', 'poly'}

Grid search will train the model for every combination of these parameters and evaluate the results.

2.2 Random Search

Random search randomly samples combinations of hyperparameters from a defined search space. It is often faster than grid search because it doesn't exhaustively search all possible combinations but instead samples randomly. Random search has been shown to work well in practice, especially when there are many hyperparameters and when only a subset of combinations will yield the best results.

- **Advantages of Random Search**:
    - It can discover better combinations in less time.
    - It is often more effective when some hyperparameters do not have a significant effect on model performance.

For instance, if we have a continuous range of possible values for CCC and gamma in an SVM, random search might sample values from a specified range, like C∈[0.01,10]C \in [0.01, 10]C∈[0.01,10] and γ∈[0.001,1]\gamma \in [0.001, 1]γ∈[0.001,1].

---

3. Scikit-learn's GridSearchCV and RandomizedSearchCV

Scikit-learn provides built-in functions for hyperparameter tuning: **GridSearchCV** and **RandomizedSearchCV**. Both perform an exhaustive search over a grid of parameters, but with different approaches for sampling and testing.

3.1 GridSearchCV

GridSearchCV performs an exhaustive search over a specified parameter grid. It evaluates all possible combinations of the hyperparameters, and you can also specify cross-validation to assess each combination's performance.

Example syntax:

```python

from sklearn.model_selection import GridSearchCV
from sklearn.svm import SVC

# Define model
svm_model = SVC()

# Define hyperparameter grid
param_grid = {'C': [0.1, 1, 10], 'kernel': ['linear', 'rbf']}
```

```
# Setup GridSearchCV
grid_search      =      GridSearchCV(estimator=svm_model,
param_grid=param_grid, cv=5)


# Fit model with grid search
grid_search.fit(X_train, y_train)


# Best parameters and score
print("Best parameters:", grid_search.best_params_)
print("Best          cross-validation          score:",
grid_search.best_score_)
```

3.2 RandomizedSearchCV

`RandomizedSearchCV` samples hyperparameters from a given distribution. It is more efficient when the hyperparameter space is large and you want to quickly find a good solution.

Example syntax:

```
python


from          sklearn.model_selection          import
RandomizedSearchCV
from sklearn.svm import SVC
from scipy.stats import uniform


# Define model
svm_model = SVC()


# Define hyperparameter distributions
```

```
param_dist = {'C': uniform(0.1, 10), 'gamma':
uniform(0.001, 1), 'kernel': ['linear', 'rbf']}

# Setup RandomizedSearchCV
random_search                                    =
RandomizedSearchCV(estimator=svm_model,
param_distributions=param_dist, n_iter=100, cv=5)

# Fit model with random search
random_search.fit(X_train, y_train)

# Best parameters and score
print("Best parameters:", random_search.best_params_)
print("Best          cross-validation          score:",
random_search.best_score_)
```

---

4. Real-World Example: Tuning Hyperparameters for an SVM Model to Predict Churn

In this example, we will use **Support Vector Machine (SVM)** to predict whether a customer will churn or not, based on their usage data. SVM is a powerful classifier, but its performance heavily depends on the right choice of hyperparameters, such as the regularization parameter CCC and the kernel function.

4.1 Problem Setup

Let's say we have a dataset where each row represents a customer, and the features include their age, monthly usage, and customer support interactions. The target variable indicates whether the customer has churned (1) or not (0).

4.2 Hyperparameter Tuning Steps

1. **Step 1: Define the Hyperparameter Grid**
   We will define a grid of possible values for CCC (regularization parameter) and kernel type, and use **GridSearchCV** to find the best combination.
2. **Step 2: Set up GridSearchCV**
   We will use 5-fold cross-validation to evaluate each combination of hyperparameters.
3. **Step 3: Fit the Model and Evaluate**
   After running the grid search, we will print the best combination of hyperparameters and assess the model's accuracy.

Example:

python

```
from sklearn.svm import SVC
from sklearn.model_selection import GridSearchCV
from sklearn.datasets import load_iris

# Load dataset (replace with churn dataset in
practice)
data = load_iris()
X, y = data.data, data.target
```

```
# Define model
svm_model = SVC()

# Define hyperparameter grid
param_grid = {'C': [0.1, 1, 10], 'kernel': ['linear',
'rbf']}

# Setup GridSearchCV
grid_search      =      GridSearchCV(estimator=svm_model,
param_grid=param_grid, cv=5)

# Fit model
grid_search.fit(X, y)

# Best parameters and score
print("Best parameters:", grid_search.best_params_)
print("Best          cross-validation          score:",
grid_search.best_score_)
```

4.3 Results Interpretation

- The best parameters might be C=1C = 1C=1 and kernel type 'rbf'.
- The model might achieve a **cross-validation score** of 0.95, indicating excellent generalization.

4.4 Refining Further with RandomizedSearchCV

If we want to explore a larger hyperparameter space but have limited computational resources, we might switch to

RandomizedSearchCV and explore a broader range of values for CCC and γ\gamma$\gamma$, leading to faster convergence.

5.

Hyperparameter tuning is an essential step in optimizing machine learning models. By using tools like **GridSearchCV** and **RandomizedSearchCV**, we can systematically explore the hyperparameter space and find the best combination of values to improve model performance. In the real-world example of churn prediction, we learned how to tune an SVM model, resulting in better generalization and higher prediction accuracy.

Chapter 18: Ensemble Learning: Boosting and Bagging

Ensemble learning involves combining multiple models to produce a stronger, more accurate model. The idea is that by leveraging the diversity of multiple models, we can reduce the errors that any individual model might make, leading to improved performance. This chapter introduces key ensemble learning techniques, including **bagging, boosting,** and **stacking,** and focuses on two popular ensemble methods: **Random Forests** and **Gradient Boosting**. We will discuss **when and why** to use ensemble methods and apply a **Random Forest** model to a real-world problem, **fraud detection**.

---

1. What is Ensemble Learning?

Ensemble learning combines predictions from multiple models to create a more accurate and robust model. The basic idea is that a group of weak learners (models that perform only slightly better than random guessing) can be combined to form a strong learner.

Ensemble methods typically fall into two broad categories:

- **Bagging (Bootstrap Aggregating)**: Reduces variance by averaging predictions from multiple models trained on different subsets of the data.

- **Boosting**: Reduces bias by sequentially training models where each subsequent model corrects the errors of the previous one.

Both bagging and boosting aim to improve the performance of machine learning algorithms by combining multiple models to reduce overfitting (in the case of bagging) or underfitting (in the case of boosting).

---

2. Bagging: Reducing Variance

2.1 Random Forests

Random Forests is one of the most popular bagging algorithms. It builds multiple decision trees on different bootstrapped subsets of the data and averages their predictions to reduce overfitting and improve generalization. Each tree in the random forest is trained on a different subset of the data, and only a random subset of features is used to make splits at each node. The combination of these multiple trees provides a more robust and stable model.

- **Key Features**:
  - **Bootstrapping**: Each tree is trained on a random subset of the data (with replacement).
  - **Random feature selection**: At each node, a random subset of features is considered for

splitting the data, which helps to create diverse trees.

- **When to Use**:
  - When you have a large dataset with many features.
  - When you want to reduce overfitting but still maintain a high degree of model complexity.
  - When interpretability is less of a priority, but predictive performance is crucial.

2.2 Real-World Example: Fraud Detection with Random Forest

For fraud detection, a random forest can be an excellent choice because it can handle complex, non-linear patterns in high-dimensional data. Fraudulent transactions often involve intricate relationships that are not easily captured by simple models.

- **Steps**:
  1. **Data Preparation**: Import data on credit card transactions, including features like transaction amount, location, time, and merchant.
  2. **Feature Engineering**: Generate new features that might indicate fraud, such as unusual transaction frequency or abnormal transaction patterns.

3. **Model Training**: Use `RandomForestClassifier` in Scikit-learn to train the model on the transaction dataset.

4. **Evaluation**: Assess model performance using metrics such as **accuracy**, **precision**, **recall**, and **F1-score** to ensure the model correctly identifies fraudulent transactions without raising too many false alarms.

```python
from sklearn.ensemble import RandomForestClassifier
from sklearn.model_selection import train_test_split
from sklearn.metrics import classification_report

# Sample dataset (fraudulent transactions)
X = data.drop('fraud_label', axis=1)
y = data['fraud_label']

# Split the data
X_train,      X_test,      y_train,      y_test      =
train_test_split(X,            y,            test_size=0.2,
random_state=42)

# Train the Random Forest model
rf_model   =   RandomForestClassifier(n_estimators=100,
random_state=42)
rf_model.fit(X_train, y_train)
```

```
# Evaluate the model
y_pred = rf_model.predict(X_test)
print(classification_report(y_test, y_pred))
```

In this example, the random forest model is likely to perform better than a single decision tree because it reduces overfitting, handles noisy features, and is less sensitive to outliers.

---

3. Boosting: Reducing Bias

3.1 Gradient Boosting

Gradient Boosting is a boosting algorithm that builds an ensemble of weak learners (typically shallow decision trees) sequentially, where each tree corrects the errors of the previous one. Each new tree is trained to predict the residuals (errors) from the previous trees, rather than the target variable itself.

- **Key Features**:
    - **Sequential Learning**: Trees are built one after another, with each tree correcting the errors made by the previous one.
    - **Gradient Descent**: The algorithm minimizes the loss function by fitting a new tree to the negative gradient (errors) of the existing ensemble.
- **When to Use**:

- When the dataset is not too large and you need a high-accuracy model.
- When you need to boost the performance of weak models by correcting errors iteratively.
- When you want a model that can handle both classification and regression tasks effectively.

3.2 AdaBoost (Adaptive Boosting)

AdaBoost is another boosting technique that adjusts the weights of misclassified examples so that subsequent classifiers focus more on those difficult examples. Unlike gradient boosting, AdaBoost combines the predictions of weak learners by a weighted vote, with more weight given to more accurate models.

---

4. When and Why Use Ensemble Methods?

Ensemble methods should be considered when:

- The dataset is large, and you need a robust model that can handle noise and variance.
- Your goal is to improve predictive performance by reducing errors in single models.
- You want to create models that can generalize better, especially when using high-variance models like decision trees.

5.

Ensemble learning techniques like **Random Forests** and **Gradient Boosting** can significantly improve the performance of machine learning models, especially when used in complex tasks like **fraud detection**. By combining multiple models, ensemble methods help reduce overfitting and underfitting, leading to a more accurate and robust final model.

In this chapter, we explored how **Random Forests** can be applied to real-world problems such as **fraud detection**, showcasing the power of bagging methods. In the next chapter, we will continue to explore other advanced machine learning techniques to further enhance model performance.

Chapter 19: Introduction to Unsupervised Learning

Unsupervised learning is a type of machine learning where the model is not provided with labeled data during training. Instead, the model must identify patterns and structures within the data on its own. This chapter will cover the basics of unsupervised learning, including the concepts of **clustering** and **dimensionality reduction**, and explain how these techniques are used in real-world scenarios, such as **customer segmentation**.

---

1. What is Unsupervised Learning?

In **supervised learning**, the model is trained using labeled data, where the desired output (target label) is already known. In contrast, **unsupervised learning** involves training a model on data that doesn't have predefined labels. The goal of unsupervised learning is to uncover hidden patterns, group similar data points together, or reduce the complexity of the data.

There are two primary categories of unsupervised learning techniques:

- **Clustering**: This technique groups data points based on similarity. The aim is to discover natural groupings in the data, such as customer segments, product categories, or topics in text.

- **Dimensionality Reduction**: This technique reduces the number of features (variables) in a dataset while preserving important relationships and patterns. It's often used to simplify datasets, improve model performance, or visualize high-dimensional data in lower-dimensional spaces.

2. Clustering: Grouping Similar Data Points

Clustering is one of the most widely used techniques in unsupervised learning. The objective is to group similar data points together so that items within each group (cluster) are more similar to each other than to items in other groups.

2.1 K-Means Clustering

One of the most common clustering algorithms is **K-Means**. This algorithm divides the data into **K** clusters by iteratively assigning each data point to the nearest cluster center and adjusting the centers based on the assigned points.

- **Steps**:
    1. Choose the number of clusters KKK.
    2. Randomly initialize the K cluster centroids.
    3. Assign each data point to the nearest centroid.

4. Recalculate the centroids as the mean of all data points in each cluster.

5. Repeat the process until the centroids no longer change significantly.

2.2 Real-World Example: Customer Segmentation

Customer segmentation is a common application of clustering in business, where businesses group customers based on similarities in purchasing behavior, demographics, or interactions with the company. This can help marketers target specific customer segments with tailored products or campaigns.

- **Steps**:
    1. **Data Preparation**: Start by collecting customer data, such as age, gender, transaction history, and purchase frequency.
    2. **Feature Selection**: Choose relevant features for segmentation, such as total spending, frequency of purchases, and product categories purchased.
    3. **Clustering with K-Means**: Use the K-Means algorithm to segment customers into groups that exhibit similar purchasing behavior.
    4. **Analysis**: Interpret the clusters to identify common characteristics of each group (e.g.,

high spenders, frequent buyers, one-time purchasers).

python

```python
from sklearn.cluster import KMeans
import pandas as pd

# Sample customer data (Age, Total Spending,
Frequency of Purchase)
data = pd.DataFrame({
    'Age': [25, 40, 35, 60, 22, 30],
    'Total_Spending': [500, 1200, 800, 300, 400,
650],
    'Frequency': [5, 20, 10, 3, 4, 6]
})

# Fit K-Means model
kmeans = KMeans(n_clusters=2, random_state=42)
data['Cluster'] = kmeans.fit_predict(data)

# View results
print(data)
```

In this example, the customers are grouped based on their age, total spending, and purchase frequency. The clustering result helps the business identify which customers are high spenders and which ones are infrequent buyers.

2.3 Other Clustering Algorithms

- **Hierarchical Clustering**: Unlike K-Means, hierarchical clustering doesn't require specifying the number of clusters beforehand. It builds a tree of clusters based on the data's similarities.
- **DBSCAN**: Density-based spatial clustering of applications with noise (DBSCAN) identifies clusters of varying shapes and sizes, making it effective for datasets with noise and outliers.

---

3. Dimensionality Reduction: Reducing Data Complexity

Dimensionality reduction is the process of reducing the number of input features (variables) while maintaining the essential information. This is particularly useful when dealing with datasets that have a large number of features, which may introduce noise and computational complexity.

3.1 Principal Component Analysis (PCA)

PCA is a statistical technique that transforms data into a smaller set of orthogonal components that capture the most variance in the data. It's a powerful method for reducing the dimensionality of a dataset while preserving as much information as possible.

- **Steps**:
    1. Standardize the data (mean = 0, variance = 1).

2. Compute the covariance matrix to understand how features vary with one another.

3. Calculate the eigenvalues and eigenvectors of the covariance matrix.

4. Sort the eigenvectors by eigenvalue magnitude and select the top kkk eigenvectors (the principal components).

5. Transform the original data by projecting it onto the top kkk eigenvectors.

3.2 Real-World Example: Reducing Complexity in Customer Data

In a scenario where a company has a dataset with hundreds of customer features (e.g., demographics, transaction history, web interactions), PCA can reduce the number of features to a manageable level while preserving key patterns.

- **Steps**:
    1. **Data Preparation**: Collect and clean data with many features (e.g., age, income, education level, purchase frequency).
    2. **Apply PCA**: Use PCA to reduce the data's dimensionality, making it easier to visualize or feed into machine learning models.
    3. **Analysis**: Analyze the top principal components to understand which combinations

of features explain the most variance in customer behavior.

python

```
from sklearn.decomposition import PCA
from sklearn.preprocessing import StandardScaler

# Standardize the data
scaler = StandardScaler()
scaled_data = scaler.fit_transform(data)

# Apply PCA to reduce dimensions
pca = PCA(n_components=2)
pca_data = pca.fit_transform(scaled_data)

# View transformed data
print(pca_data)
```

PCA helps in visualizing high-dimensional data by projecting it into two or three dimensions, enabling better insights into patterns and relationships between customers.

---

4. When and Why Use Unsupervised Learning?

Unsupervised learning is particularly useful when you:

- Don't have labeled data but still want to discover patterns or structure.

- Need to reduce the complexity of your data for further analysis or modeling (e.g., in high-dimensional spaces).
- Want to gain insights from data that might not have a clear target variable (e.g., in exploratory data analysis).
- Need to detect anomalies, trends, or clusters within the data (e.g., fraud detection, customer segmentation).

5.

Unsupervised learning techniques such as clustering and dimensionality reduction are vital tools in the data scientist's toolkit. By grouping similar data points together or reducing the number of features in a dataset, unsupervised learning helps uncover hidden patterns, simplify complex data, and provide insights for further analysis. Whether it's for **customer segmentation** or **fraud detection**, these techniques offer valuable solutions to real-world problems.

Chapter 20: Clustering with k-Means

Clustering with **k-Means** is one of the most popular unsupervised learning techniques used to group similar data points together. In this chapter, we will explore the **k-Means** algorithm in more depth, including how to implement it in Python, determine the optimal number of clusters, and apply it to a real-world example, such as grouping customers based on their buying patterns.

---

1. Understanding the k-Means Algorithm

The **k-Means** algorithm is a type of **partitioning** clustering algorithm that divides data into KKK non-overlapping clusters, where KKK is specified in advance. The primary objective of k-Means is to minimize the variance within each cluster while maximizing the variance between clusters. The algorithm works iteratively to find the best cluster centroids that minimize the sum of squared distances between data points and their corresponding centroids.

Steps Involved in k-Means:

1. **Initialization**: Randomly select KKK data points as the initial centroids.
2. **Assignment Step**: Assign each data point to the nearest centroid. This creates KKK clusters.

3. **Update Step**: Recalculate the centroids of the clusters by averaging the data points assigned to each cluster.

4. **Repeat**: Repeat the assignment and update steps until the centroids no longer change significantly (i.e., convergence).

---

2. Implementing k-Means in Python

Python's **Scikit-learn** library provides a simple and efficient implementation of the k-Means algorithm. Below is an example of how to apply k-Means clustering using Python:

Step-by-Step Guide to Implementing k-Means:

1. **Import Required Libraries**: You need `pandas` for data handling, `matplotlib` for visualization, and `sklearn` for the k-Means algorithm.

2. **Prepare the Data**: Load the data that you want to cluster. This can be any dataset, such as customer purchase data, product features, or even image data.

3. **Apply k-Means Clustering**: Use the `KMeans` class from **Scikit-learn** to fit the model and predict cluster labels.

4. **Visualize the Clusters**: After fitting the model, visualize the clusters using a scatter plot or any other appropriate visualization technique.

Here is a Python code example to implement k-Means:

```python
python

import pandas as pd
from sklearn.cluster import KMeans
import matplotlib.pyplot as plt

# Sample data: Customer purchase data (age, income)
data = pd.DataFrame({
    'Age': [25, 45, 35, 50, 23, 35, 40, 60, 30, 70],
    'Income': [50000, 120000, 80000, 100000, 40000,
65000, 90000, 150000, 60000, 200000]
})

# Fit the KMeans model with 3 clusters
kmeans = KMeans(n_clusters=3, random_state=42)
data['Cluster']    =    kmeans.fit_predict(data[['Age',
'Income']])

# Plotting the results
plt.scatter(data['Age'],                data['Income'],
c=data['Cluster'], cmap='viridis')
plt.xlabel('Age')
plt.ylabel('Income')
plt.title('Customer Segmentation Using k-Means')
plt.show()
```

In this example, the model segments customers based on their age and income, and the scatter plot visualizes the three clusters formed by the algorithm.

3. Determining the Optimal Number of Clusters

Choosing the right number of clusters, KKK, is a critical part of applying k-Means clustering. If KKK is too small, the algorithm might oversimplify the data. If KKK is too large, it might overfit the data and create meaningless clusters.

3.1 Elbow Method

The **Elbow Method** is one of the most commonly used techniques to determine the optimal value of KKK. The method involves plotting the **within-cluster sum of squares (WCSS)**, which measures the compactness of the clusters. As KKK increases, the WCSS will decrease. The idea is to find the "elbow" point where the decrease in WCSS starts to slow down. This point is considered the optimal number of clusters.

Steps for the Elbow Method:

1. Fit the k-Means algorithm for different values of KKK.
2. Calculate the WCSS for each KKK.
3. Plot the WCSS against KKK and look for the "elbow" point.

python

```python
# Elbow Method for finding optimal K
wcss = []
```

```
for k in range(1, 11):   # Try values of K from 1 to
10
    kmeans = KMeans(n_clusters=k, random_state=42)
    kmeans.fit(data[['Age', 'Income']])
    wcss.append(kmeans.inertia_)

# Plot the WCSS
plt.plot(range(1, 11), wcss)
plt.title('Elbow Method for Optimal K')
plt.xlabel('Number of Clusters')
plt.ylabel('WCSS')
plt.show()
```

The plot will help identify the optimal number of clusters KKK by locating the "elbow," where the decrease in WCSS starts to level off.

3.2 Silhouette Score

Another method to evaluate the clustering performance is the **Silhouette Score**, which measures how similar each point is to its own cluster compared to other clusters. The silhouette score ranges from -1 to +1, where +1 indicates well-defined clusters, 0 indicates overlapping clusters, and negative values suggest that points may have been assigned to the wrong clusters.

```python

from sklearn.metrics import silhouette_score

# Calculate silhouette score for k=3
```

181

```
score   =   silhouette_score(data[['Age',   'Income']],
data['Cluster'])
print(f"Silhouette Score for k=3: {score}")
```

4. Real-World Example: Grouping Customers Based on Their Buying Patterns

Clustering can be extremely valuable in business applications. For example, companies often use k-Means clustering to group customers based on their purchasing behavior. By analyzing these clusters, businesses can tailor their marketing strategies, optimize inventory, and personalize product recommendations.

Steps for Customer Segmentation:

1. **Data Preparation**: Collect customer data, such as transaction history, purchase frequency, product preferences, and demographic details.
2. **Feature Selection**: Select relevant features, such as total spending, average purchase frequency, and categories of products purchased.
3. **Apply k-Means**: Use the k-Means algorithm to segment customers into different groups (e.g., high spenders, occasional buyers, low spenders).
4. **Analysis**: Interpret the clusters and develop targeted marketing campaigns for each customer segment.

```python
# Sample customer data (total spending, purchase
frequency)
customer_data = pd.DataFrame({
    'Spending': [100, 250, 300, 150, 50, 80, 200,
500, 60, 400],
    'Frequency': [5, 20, 18, 10, 3, 4, 15, 30, 5, 25]
})

# Apply k-Means clustering
kmeans = KMeans(n_clusters=3, random_state=42)
customer_data['Segment']                          =
kmeans.fit_predict(customer_data[['Spending',
'Frequency']])

# Visualize customer segments
plt.scatter(customer_data['Spending'],
customer_data['Frequency'],
c=customer_data['Segment'], cmap='viridis')
plt.xlabel('Total Spending')
plt.ylabel('Purchase Frequency')
plt.title('Customer Segmentation Using k-Means')
plt.show()
```

By segmenting customers, businesses can identify high-value customers for targeted promotions, while also detecting low-engagement customers who may need special attention.

5.

k-Means clustering is a powerful tool for grouping data points based on similarity. By using the Elbow method or Silhouette Score, you can determine the optimal number of clusters, leading to meaningful insights. Whether it's for customer segmentation, marketing strategies, or fraud detection, clustering provides valuable patterns that can drive business decisions and improve predictive models.

Chapter 21: Hierarchical Clustering: Building a Dendrogram

Hierarchical clustering is another popular unsupervised learning technique used for clustering data. Unlike **k-Means** clustering, which requires specifying the number of clusters beforehand, hierarchical clustering creates a hierarchy of clusters and doesn't require this prior specification. This chapter will cover the principles of **hierarchical clustering**, how to build a **dendrogram** (a tree-like diagram that shows the hierarchical relationship between clusters), and demonstrate its application through a real-world example of **segmenting products based on customer preferences**.

---

1. What is Hierarchical Clustering?

Hierarchical clustering is a method of clustering that builds a tree of clusters. It starts by treating each data point as its own individual cluster and then progressively merges the closest clusters together until only one cluster remains.

There are two main types of hierarchical clustering:

- **Agglomerative Clustering**: This is the most common form of hierarchical clustering, where each data point starts as its own cluster, and pairs of clusters are merged iteratively based on a distance metric.

- **Divisive Clustering**: This is a top-down approach where all data points start in one cluster, and the cluster is recursively split into smaller clusters.

For this chapter, we will focus on **agglomerative clustering**, as it is most commonly used in practice.

---

2. How Agglomerative Hierarchical Clustering Works

The process of **agglomerative clustering** can be described as follows:

1. **Initialization**: Each data point is treated as its own cluster.

2. **Distance Calculation**: The distance (or similarity) between all clusters is calculated. The most common distance metric used is **Euclidean distance**, but others like **Manhattan** or **Cosine similarity** can also be used.

3. **Cluster Merging**: The two closest clusters are merged into a new cluster.

4. **Repeat**: Steps 2 and 3 are repeated until all points are in a single cluster. The result is a **dendrogram**, a

tree-like diagram that shows the hierarchy of the clusters and their relationships.

The algorithm stops when all points are in one cluster, but the key benefit is that it allows the user to cut the dendrogram at any point to choose the number of clusters they want.

---

3. Building a Dendrogram

A **dendrogram** is a tree-like diagram that visually represents the results of hierarchical clustering. It shows how clusters are merged together at each step of the algorithm, and it allows you to decide on the optimal number of clusters by cutting the dendrogram at a particular level.

Steps to Create a Dendrogram:

1. Perform hierarchical clustering using a distance metric (e.g., **Euclidean distance**).
2. Generate the dendrogram to visualize the cluster hierarchy.
3. Cut the dendrogram at the appropriate level to define the desired number of clusters.

Python Code Example: Hierarchical Clustering with Dendrogram

python

```python
import pandas as pd
from sklearn.cluster import AqqlomerativeClustering
import matplotlib.pyplot as plt
import seaborn as sns
from scipy.cluster.hierarchy import dendrogram, linkage

# Sample data: Product preferences (Customer rating
for products A, B, C)
data = pd.DataFrame({
    'Product_A': [5, 4, 3, 2, 4, 5],
    'Product_B': [2, 3, 4, 5, 3, 2],
    'Product_C': [4, 5, 4, 2, 5, 4]
})

# Perform hierarchical clustering using the 'ward'
linkage method
Z = linkage(data, method='ward')

# Plot the dendrogram
plt.figure(figsize=(10, 7))
dendrogram(Z)
plt.title('Dendrogram for Hierarchical Clustering')
plt.xlabel('Products')
plt.ylabel('Euclidean Distance')
plt.show()
```

In this example:

- **Linkage Method**: We used the `ward` linkage method, which minimizes the variance within each cluster. Other linkage methods include `single` and `complete`, which define distance differently between clusters.
- **Dendrogram**: The plot visualizes how products are grouped together based on their similarity. You can cut the dendrogram at a certain level to define the number of clusters.

---

4. Real-World Example: Segmenting Products Based on Customer Preferences

In business, **segmentation** is used to group products that share similar customer preferences. This helps companies identify trends, optimize product assortments, or design targeted marketing strategies.

Example Scenario: Segmenting Products Based on Customer Preferences

Suppose a company sells a variety of products, and they want to group these products based on customer preferences to identify which products tend to be bought together or appeal to similar customer groups. We have a dataset where each product is rated by customers on various features (e.g., quality, design, price).

Steps to Implement Product Segmentation Using Hierarchical Clustering:

1. **Data Preparation**: Gather the ratings or purchase data for products (e.g., customer ratings of products in different categories).

2. **Clustering**: Perform hierarchical clustering using the `ward` method (or another method) to group similar products.

3. **Interpretation**: Analyze the dendrogram to decide on the number of clusters. For example, you may decide to cut the dendrogram at a point that creates 3 product clusters.

4. **Actionable Insights**: Use the resulting clusters to make decisions about inventory management, marketing, or customer targeting. For instance, products in the same cluster might be marketed together or displayed in proximity in stores.

---

5. Advantages of Hierarchical Clustering

- **No Need to Pre-define the Number of Clusters**: Unlike k-Means, hierarchical clustering doesn't require the user to specify the number of clusters upfront.

- **Flexible**: The dendrogram allows you to explore different clustering solutions by cutting it at various levels.
- **Intuitive**: The results are easy to interpret and visualize through the dendrogram, which makes hierarchical clustering more interpretable than some other methods.

---

6. Limitations of Hierarchical Clustering

- **Scalability**: Hierarchical clustering can be computationally expensive for large datasets. It has a time complexity of $O(n3)O(n^3)O(n3)$, which makes it less efficient for very large datasets.
- **Sensitive to Noise and Outliers**: Hierarchical clustering can be sensitive to noise, which might affect the final clusters.

7.

Hierarchical clustering is a powerful tool for grouping data without needing predefined labels. By building a dendrogram, it allows users to visualize the clustering process and make informed decisions about the number of clusters. In the real-world example of **segmenting products based on customer preferences**, hierarchical clustering provides valuable insights that can help optimize product offerings and marketing strategies.

Chapter 22: Principal Component Analysis (PCA)

Principal Component Analysis (PCA) is a powerful technique used in unsupervised learning for **dimensionality reduction**. It helps reduce the complexity of high-dimensional datasets by transforming them into a smaller set of dimensions (called **principal components**) while retaining as much of the original variance as possible. This chapter will cover how to apply PCA for dimensionality reduction, how to visualize high-dimensional data in lower dimensions, and provide a real-world example of reducing the dimensions of a dataset for improved visualization.

---

1. What is Principal Component Analysis (PCA)?

PCA is a statistical method that transforms a large set of correlated variables into a smaller set of uncorrelated variables, known as **principal components**. These principal components represent the directions of maximum variance in the data.

Key Concepts in PCA:

- **Principal Components**: These are new variables that are linear combinations of the original variables, chosen so that the first principal component captures the greatest variance, the second captures the second greatest variance, and so on.

- **Dimensionality Reduction**: PCA reduces the number of features in the data by selecting only the most important principal components, which helps simplify models and improves computational efficiency.
- **Variance**: In PCA, we aim to preserve as much variance as possible when reducing dimensions, ensuring that the most important patterns in the data remain.

PCA is especially useful when dealing with datasets that have many features (high-dimensional data) and when there is multicollinearity (i.e., many features are correlated with one another).

---

2. How PCA Works

The process of PCA can be broken down into the following steps:

1. **Standardize the Data**:
   - PCA is affected by the scale of the data, so it's important to standardize the data so that each feature has zero mean and unit variance.
2. **Compute the Covariance Matrix**:

- o The covariance matrix represents how each feature in the dataset relates to the others. It gives us an understanding of the relationships between features.

3. **Calculate the Eigenvalues and Eigenvectors**:
    - o The eigenvectors represent the directions of maximum variance (the principal components), while the eigenvalues tell us how much variance is captured by each principal component.

4. **Sort the Eigenvalues and Eigenvectors**:
    - o Sort the eigenvalues in descending order to determine the importance of each principal component.

5. **Choose the Top k Principal Components**:
    - o Select the top k eigenvectors corresponding to the largest eigenvalues, where k is the number of dimensions you want to reduce to.

6. **Transform the Data**:
    - o The final step is to project the original data onto the selected eigenvectors, reducing its dimensionality.

---

3. *Visualizing High-Dimensional Data with PCA*

One of the primary benefits of PCA is its ability to reduce high-dimensional data to two or three dimensions, allowing for easier visualization. By projecting the data onto the first two or three principal components, we can create scatter plots that show the structure of the data.

Visualizing Data:

- When you reduce data to two or three dimensions, you can plot it on a 2D or 3D scatter plot, making it easier to identify patterns, clusters, and outliers.
- PCA can also help reveal underlying relationships and correlations between features that might be hard to spot in a high-dimensional space.

---

4. Applying PCA in Python with Scikit-learn

Scikit-learn provides a simple and efficient way to implement PCA. Below is an example of how to apply PCA to a dataset, reduce its dimensionality, and visualize the result.

Step-by-Step Guide to Implementing PCA:

1. **Import Necessary Libraries**: You will need `pandas` for handling the data, `scikit-learn` for PCA, and `matplotlib` for visualization.

2. **Standardize the Data**: PCA requires that the data be standardized before applying the technique.

3. **Fit the PCA Model**: Use the PCA class in Scikit-learn to fit the model and transform the data into principal components.

4. **Visualize the Results**: Plot the first two principal components to visualize the reduced dataset.

Python Code Example: PCA for Dimensionality Reduction

```python
import pandas as pd
from sklearn.decomposition import PCA
from sklearn.preprocessing import StandardScaler
import matplotlib.pyplot as plt

# Sample data: 4 features (e.g., features related to
product attributes)
data = pd.DataFrame({
    'Feature1': [1, 2, 3, 4, 5, 6],
    'Feature2': [2, 3, 4, 5, 6, 7],
    'Feature3': [5, 6, 7, 8, 9, 10],
    'Feature4': [10, 9, 8, 7, 6, 5]
})

# Standardizing the data
scaler = StandardScaler()
data_scaled = scaler.fit_transform(data)
```

```
# Applying PCA to reduce the data to 2 dimensions
pca = PCA(n_components=2)
pca_result = pca.fit_transform(data_scaled)

# Plotting the first two principal components
plt.figure(figsize=(8, 6))
plt.scatter(pca_result[:,    0],    pca_result[:,    1],
c='blue', label='Data Points')
plt.title('PCA:    2D    Projection    of    High-Dimensional
Data')
plt.xlabel('Principal Component 1')
plt.ylabel('Principal Component 2')
plt.legend()
plt.show()
```

In this example:

- **Standardizing Data**: We first scale the data using StandardScaler to ensure that each feature has zero mean and unit variance.
- **Applying PCA**: The PCA function is used to reduce the data to 2 dimensions (for visualization purposes).
- **Plotting**: The resulting data is then visualized on a 2D scatter plot.

---

5. Real-World Example: Reducing Dimensions for Improved Visualization

In this real-world example, imagine that you are analyzing customer data with several features, such as **age**, **income**, **spending habits**, and **product preferences**. The dataset has many features, and visualizing them directly is difficult due to the high dimensionality. By applying PCA, we can reduce the dataset to two or three dimensions and create a visual representation that is much easier to analyze.

Steps:

1. **Data Preparation**: You import the customer dataset containing multiple features.
2. **Dimensionality Reduction**: Use PCA to reduce the features down to two principal components.
3. **Visualization**: Plot the transformed data on a scatter plot, which can reveal clusters of similar customers or patterns that were previously hidden.

For example, PCA could show that customers who prefer high-end products tend to cluster in a certain region of the 2D space, while budget-conscious customers form another cluster.

6.

PCA is a powerful tool for dimensionality reduction, particularly in high-dimensional datasets. By reducing the number of features while preserving the variance in the data, PCA helps make analysis more manageable and allows for better data visualization. In this chapter, we have discussed how PCA works, how to implement it using Python and Scikit-learn, and demonstrated its application through a real-world example of reducing dimensions for improved visualization.

Understanding and applying PCA effectively can dramatically improve the clarity of your analysis, especially when dealing with complex, high-dimensional data.

Chapter 23: Deep Learning and Neural Networks

Deep Learning is a subset of machine learning that deals with neural networks, which are algorithms inspired by the structure and function of the human brain. Deep learning has revolutionized fields like computer vision, natural language processing, and predictive analytics due to its ability to automatically learn complex patterns from large datasets. In this chapter, we will explore the concepts behind **neural networks**, **backpropagation**, and **activation functions**, and show how to implement a neural network using popular frameworks such as **Keras** and **TensorFlow** in Python. We will also demonstrate a **real-world example** of building a neural network to predict **customer churn**.

---

1. Introduction to Deep Learning Concepts

Deep learning is primarily built upon the concept of **neural networks**—mathematical models that are capable of learning and performing tasks such as classification, regression, and pattern recognition by simulating the behavior of the human brain.

Neural Networks Overview:

- **Neurons**: A neural network is composed of layers of neurons, which are units that perform mathematical operations on the data. Each neuron receives inputs, applies weights, adds a bias, and passes the result through an activation function to produce an output.

- **Layers**: A neural network consists of multiple layers:
  - o **Input layer**: The first layer that takes input features.
  - o **Hidden layers**: Intermediate layers where computations are performed to learn features.
  - o **Output layer**: The final layer that outputs predictions or classifications.

Neural networks can have many layers, hence the term **deep learning**. Networks with more layers are capable of learning more complex patterns.

Backpropagation:

- Backpropagation is the process of training neural networks. It involves adjusting the weights of the network by calculating the error between the predicted output and the actual output, then propagating this error back through the network to update the weights. This allows the network to **learn from its mistakes** and improve its predictions.

Activation Functions:

- **Activation functions** introduce non-linearity into the network, allowing it to model complex patterns. Without activation functions, neural networks would only be able to model linear relationships. Common activation functions include:
  - **Sigmoid**: Outputs a value between 0 and 1, often used in binary classification.
  - **ReLU (Rectified Linear Unit)**: Allows for faster training and helps mitigate the vanishing gradient problem, often used in hidden layers.
  - **Softmax**: Used in the output layer of multi-class classification problems to convert raw output into probabilities.

---

2. Using Keras and TensorFlow for Building Neural Networks in Python

Keras is an open-source deep learning framework written in Python that runs on top of **TensorFlow**, a more comprehensive deep learning library. Keras makes it easy to define and train neural networks with simple, high-level APIs.

Installing Keras and TensorFlow:

To start building neural networks, you first need to install **TensorFlow** (which includes Keras) using `pip`:

```bash
```

```
pip install tensorflow
```

Building a Simple Neural Network in Keras:

Let's walk through the process of building a neural network using **Keras** and **TensorFlow** for a customer churn prediction problem.

1. **Prepare the Data**:
   - For this example, we'll use a dataset of customer information, with features like `age`, `gender`, `income`, and `product usage`. The target variable (y) is whether or not the customer churned (binary classification).

2. **Define the Model**:
   - We'll create a simple neural network with an input layer, one hidden layer, and an output layer.

3. **Compile the Model**:
   - We need to define the loss function, optimizer, and evaluation metric for training.

4. **Train the Model**:
   - Finally, we'll fit the model to the data and evaluate its performance.

Example Code: Building a Neural Network to Predict Customer Churn

```python

import tensorflow as tf
from tensorflow.keras.models import Sequential
from tensorflow.keras.layers import Dense
from tensorflow.keras.optimizers import Adam
import pandas as pd
import numpy as np

# Sample data: Customer features and churn status (1:
Churn, 0: No Churn)
data = pd.DataFrame({
    'age': [25, 45, 35, 50, 23],
    'income': [40000, 120000, 80000, 110000, 25000],
    'product_usage': [5, 7, 6, 8, 2],
    'churn': [0, 0, 1, 0, 1]  # Churn target variable
})

# Features and target variable
X = data[['age', 'income', 'product_usage']].values
y = data['churn'].values

# Define the model
model = Sequential()
model.add(Dense(8,                input_dim=X.shape[1],
activation='relu'))  # Hidden layer with 8 neurons
model.add(Dense(1, activation='sigmoid'))   # Output
layer (sigmoid for binary classification)

# Compile the model
```

```python
model.compile(optimizer=Adam(),
loss='binary_crossentropy', metrics=['accuracy'])

# Train the model
model.fit(X, y, epochs=50, batch_size=1, verbose=1)

# Evaluate the model
loss, accuracy = model.evaluate(X, y)
print(f'Model Accuracy: {accuracy * 100:.2f}%')

# Making predictions
predictions = model.predict(X)
print("Predictions:", predictions)
```

In this example:

- We created a neural network with one hidden layer containing 8 neurons and an output layer with a sigmoid activation function for binary classification (churn vs. no churn).
- We used the **Adam** optimizer, which is efficient and commonly used for training neural networks.
- **Binary cross-entropy** is used as the loss function for binary classification problems.

---

3. Real-World Example: Building a Neural Network to Predict Customer Churn

Problem Definition: Imagine you work for a telecom company and want to predict whether a customer is likely to churn (i.e., cancel their subscription). Predicting churn can help the company take proactive measures to retain customers, such as offering discounts or special services.

Dataset: The dataset contains customer information such as age, income, usage patterns, and whether they have churned in the past.

Steps:

1. **Data Preprocessing**: The dataset might require cleaning (handling missing values, encoding categorical variables, scaling features).
2. **Model Building**: A neural network is defined with appropriate layers, optimizers, and activation functions.
3. **Training**: The model is trained on the data using backpropagation.
4. **Model Evaluation**: The performance is evaluated using accuracy, precision, recall, and other metrics.

Benefits:

- Neural networks can capture complex non-linear patterns in the data that simpler models (e.g., decision trees or logistic regression) may miss.

- By leveraging deep learning, you can improve the accuracy of your churn prediction model, which helps the company make better decisions for customer retention.

4.

Deep learning, through neural networks, offers a powerful tool for solving complex problems in areas such as customer churn prediction, image recognition, and natural language processing. With libraries like **Keras** and **TensorFlow**, it's easier than ever to implement neural networks in Python and leverage their capabilities for real-world applications. By understanding the key concepts behind neural networks—such as backpropagation, activation functions, and how to train and evaluate a model— you'll be able to design and deploy deep learning models that can tackle a wide range of machine learning problems.

Chapter 24: Deploying Machine Learning Models

Deploying machine learning models into production is the process of taking a trained model and making it available for real-world use. This involves setting up an environment where the model can make predictions in response to incoming data, often via an API or web interface. In this chapter, we will cover the process of deploying machine learning models, creating **APIs with Flask**, and hosting models on the **cloud**. We'll walk through a real-world example of deploying a model that predicts **employee turnover** as a web service.

---

1. Overview of Deploying Machine Learning Models

Once you've trained a machine learning model, it's essential to make it available for production environments, where it can be used to make real-time predictions. Model deployment is crucial for turning machine learning prototypes into tangible products that end-users can interact with.

Steps in the Deployment Process:

1. **Model Exporting**:

o After training the model, export it in a format suitable for deployment (e.g., `.pkl` for Python, `.h5` for Keras models).

2. **API Creation**:

   o Create an API (Application Programming Interface) so that other applications can send data to your model and receive predictions in response.

3. **Model Hosting**:

   o Host the model in a server environment or the cloud (e.g., AWS, Azure, Google Cloud) to make it accessible to applications and users.

4. **Real-time Prediction**:

   o Set up the model to provide real-time predictions when new data is provided.

5. **Monitoring and Updating**:

   o Once the model is deployed, continuously monitor its performance. Update it periodically to ensure it remains accurate and relevant over time as new data is collected.

---

2. Creating APIs with Flask

One of the simplest ways to deploy machine learning models is by creating a **web API**. **Flask** is a lightweight web framework for Python that can be used to turn a trained model into a web service.

Steps for Deploying a Model with Flask:

1. **Install Flask**: First, install Flask using `pip`:

   bash

   ```
   pip install flask
   ```

2. **Creating the Flask App**: Write a Flask app that exposes an endpoint where users can send data to get predictions.

   Example:

   - You might expose an endpoint `/predict`, where users can send employee data (such as age, tenure, department, etc.), and the model will return the probability of the employee leaving the company.

3. **Load the Trained Model**: Before making predictions, you need to load your trained machine learning model. You can use libraries like `joblib` or `pickle` to load the model from disk.

4. **Define a Prediction Route**: Define a route that accepts input data, processes it, and returns the prediction result.

Example Code: Building a Flask API for Model Deployment

Below is a simple example of deploying a trained machine learning model with Flask to predict employee turnover.

python

```python
import pickle
from flask import Flask, request, jsonify
import numpy as np

# Initialize Flask app
app = Flask(__name__)

# Load the trained model
model                                    =
pickle.load(open('employee_turnover_model.pkl',
'rb'))

@app.route('/')
def home():
    return "Employee Turnover Prediction API"

@app.route('/predict', methods=['POST'])
def predict():
    # Get data from POST request
    data = request.get_json(force=True)

    # Extract features from the data
    features = np.array([[
```

```
        data['age'],
        data['tenure'],
        data['salary'],
        data['department']
    ]])


    # Predict using the loaded model
    prediction = model.predict(features)


    # Return prediction as JSON
    return              jsonify({'turnover_prediction':
int(prediction[0])})


if __name__ == '__main__':
    app.run(debug=True)
```

Explanation of the Code:

- **Flask Setup**: We initialize a Flask app and define two routes: one for checking if the server is running (`/`) and another (`/predict`) that handles incoming requests for predictions.
- **Loading the Model**: The model is loaded using `pickle.load()` from a saved `.pkl` file.
- **Predict Route**: The `/predict` route accepts a POST request, extracts features from the JSON input, and passes it to the model to generate a prediction. The result is returned in JSON format.

Running the Flask Application:

To run the Flask app, save the script and run the following command:

```bash

```

```
python app.py
```

This will start a local server, and you can send POST requests to the `/predict` endpoint.

---

3. Hosting Machine Learning Models on the Cloud

Once your model is packaged into an API, the next step is to **deploy it to the cloud** to make it accessible to users across the world.

Popular Cloud Platforms for Hosting Models:

- **Amazon Web Services (AWS):**
  - AWS provides services like **Elastic Beanstalk** and **SageMaker** that are designed for deploying machine learning models.
  - You can also use **AWS Lambda** for serverless deployment, where you don't have to worry about server management.
- **Google Cloud Platform (GCP):**

- GCP offers **AI Platform** for model deployment, or you can use **Google Kubernetes Engine (GKE)** for containerized applications.
- **Cloud Functions** can be used for serverless deployments as well.

- **Microsoft Azure**:
  - Azure's **Machine Learning Service** is a robust platform for training, deploying, and managing machine learning models.
  - **Azure Functions** is a serverless compute service that can be used to deploy models.

Deploying to AWS Example:

1. **Set up an EC2 instance**: Launch a virtual server in AWS EC2 and set up your environment with the required dependencies (e.g., Flask, Python, TensorFlow).
2. **Transfer your model and API code**: Upload your trained model and Flask API code to the EC2 instance.
3. **Start the Flask app**: Use tools like **nginx** or **Gunicorn** to serve the Flask app in a production environment.
4. **Expose the API**: Configure the EC2 instance's security group to open the necessary ports (e.g., port

5000 for Flask) and ensure your API is publicly accessible.

---

4. Real-World Example: Deploying a Model to Predict Employee Turnover

For the real-world example, we will deploy a model that predicts **employee turnover**. This model takes inputs such as employee age, tenure, department, salary, and other features, then returns a prediction of whether the employee will leave the company in the next year.

Deployment Flow:

1. **Train and save the model**: We use Scikit-learn, Keras, or any other machine learning framework to train a model based on historical employee data. Once trained, the model is saved to disk (using `pickle` or `joblib`).

2. **Build the Flask API**: As shown earlier, we create a Flask API that accepts input data (e.g., employee characteristics) and uses the trained model to make predictions.

3. **Host the Flask App**: The app is deployed on a cloud service like AWS, Azure, or GCP. It is made available to HR systems or other internal tools that require real-time predictions of employee churn.

4. **Monitor the API**: Set up logging, monitoring, and automated alerts to track the API's performance, manage potential issues, and update the model as new data comes in.

Deploying machine learning models is a crucial step in making predictive models useful in real-world scenarios. By creating APIs with Flask and hosting models on the cloud, you can turn machine learning solutions into actionable tools that provide insights and predictions to users. In this chapter, you learned how to package a model into an API, deploy it to the cloud, and manage it for real-time predictions, which are essential skills for building production-ready machine learning systems.

www.ingramcontent.com/pod-product-compliance
Lightning Source LLC
LaVergne TN
LVHW051326050326
832903LV00031B/3389